READY STEADY COOK 2

RICHARD CAWLEY

PATRICK ANTHONY

PHOTOGRAPHS BY
JULIET PIDDINGTON

BBC BOOKS

This book is published to accompany the television series *Ready Steady Cook*
which was first broadcast in Autumn 1994.
The series was produced by Bazal Productions.

Published by BBC Books, an imprint of BBC Worldwide Publishing,
BBC Worldwide Ltd, Woodlands, 80 Wood Lane, London W12 0TT

First published 1996
Format © Bazal Productions
Recipes © Richard Cawley and Patrick Anthony
The moral right of the authors has been asserted.

Photographs: Juliet Piddington
Home Economist: Emma Patmore
ISBN 0 563 38757 2

Set in Futura
Designed by Louise Morley
Printed Martins the Printers Ltd, Berwick-upon-Tweed
Bound by Hunter & Foulis Ltd, Edinburgh
Colour separation by Radstock Reproductions Ltd, Midsomer Norton
Cover printed by Clays Ltd, St Ives plc

CONTENTS

INTRODUCTION

After the phenomenal success of the first *Ready Steady Cook* book, there simply had to be a follow-up, so now there are many more delicious recipes for you to prepare. If you have ever started one of our recipes, fired with enthusiasm after the show, only to find you can't remember quite how it finished, this is the book for you.

On *Ready Steady Cook* we give our chefs the ultimate culinary test. The budget is £5, the time limit is 20 minutes and, on top of all that, the ingredients are a complete surprise. Our contestants have chosen a combination of foods they love and it's the chef's job to invent a delicious recipe there and then.

These recipes make it possible for anyone to rustle up a gourmet dish. The book is full of new ideas (even the chefs surprise themselves sometimes) and it's guaranteed to inspire good and bad cooks alike.

The point is have a go – cooking is fun and the eating is even better! You can knock up a fabulous dish in 20 minutes for a fiver. Honestly. Go on – give it a try.

Presenter, *Ready Steady Cook*

A Note on Ingredients and Techniques

Good-quality ingredients make all the difference to the taste of the finished dish. For best results, choose unsalted butter and extra virgin olive oil. Buy ripe, flavoursome tomatoes, whenever possible, and really fresh herbs. If a recipe specifies dried herbs, freeze-dried ones usually have the best flavour. For desserts, chocolate should contain at least 50 per cent cocoa solids – check the back of the wrapper.

> Some of the recipes contain raw or lightly cooked eggs. Because of the slight risk of salmonella poisoning, these should be avoided by the sick, the elderly, the very young, and pregnant women.
> The chances of contamination are greatly reduced if you buy free-range eggs, preferably organic, from a reputable supplier.

Many of the recipes in this book include wine. Use a wine that you would enjoy drinking rather than cheap 'cooking' wine – if it's not worth drinking, it's not worth cooking with!

A technique favoured by the chefs on *Ready Steady Cook* is cooking on a ridged grill pan. Ridged grill pans are made of cast iron and usually have a spout for pouring off the cooking juices. They are a very healthy way of cooking because the ridges keep the food raised above any fat that runs off. They also make attractive grill marks on food – to make a criss-cross pattern, give the food a half-turn half-way through cooking each side. Use ridged grill pans for steaks, chops, fish or chunky slices of vegetables such as aubergines, courgettes or peppers.

Finally, *Ready Steady Cook* is all about putting together a delicious meal from whatever ingredients you have to hand. The recipes in this book are proof that some of the most memorable dishes are the ones that come about on the spur of the moment. So, if you don't have a particular ingredient, follow the example of our chefs and improvise. Don't be afraid to get in the kitchen and *Ready Steady Cook*!

LARDER INGREDIENTS USED ON
READY STEADY COOK

Arrowroot
Baking powder
Balsamic vinegar
Beef stock cubes
Black syrup
Bottle of red wine
Bottle of white wine
Cardamom pods
Caster sugar
Cayenne pepper
Chicken stock cubes
Cornflour
Demerara sugar
Dijon mustard
Double cream
Dried mixed herbs
Dried oregano
Eggs, size 3
Fresh basil
Fresh coriander
Fresh dill
Fresh parsley
Fresh rosemary
Fresh sage
Fresh thyme
Fresh white bread
Garam masala
Garlic
Granulated sugar

Golden syrup
Greek yoghurt
Ground all-spice
Ground cinnamon
Ground coriander
Ground ginger
Lemons/Limes
Mayonnaise
Milk
Mustard seeds
Olive oil
Oranges
Plain flour
Poppy seeds
Red wine vinegar
Self-raising flour
Sesame oil
Soft brown sugar
Soy sauce
Sunflower oil
Tabasco sauce
Tomato purée
Tomato sauce
Turmeric
Unsalted butter
Vanilla essence
Vegetable stock cubes
White wine vinegar
Wholegrain mustard

VEGETARIAN DISHES

RACHEL'S DELECTABLE THAI DREAM – 10

HAVE YOURSELF A VEGGIE LITTLE CHRISTMAS – 12

RAQUEL'S RAVISHING MUSHROOM TART – 14

DANIELLE'S CAULIFLOWER CHARMER – 15

BARBARA'S FILO DREAMBOATS – 17

MICHELLE'S MÉLANGE – 19

WENDY'S WINTER WONDER – 20

FRANCES'S FAST FEAST – 22

RICHARD CAWLEY

RACHEL'S DELECTABLE THAI DREAM

Raw and cooked vegetables, with crisp-fried and soft noodles

Rachel Morton, of Reading, is a great fan of ethnic food, from Mexican to Chinese, but she had never tasted Thai food. She asked Richard to make an authentic Thai dish with the ingredients she brought and he obliged with this beautifully balanced recipe of raw and cooked vegetables and crisp and soft noodles. The coconut and lime flavouring of the stir-fry is the essence of Thai cooking.

SERVES 2	100 g (4 oz) green beans, trimmed
4 carrots	1 garlic clove, crushed
4 spring onions	1 fresh red chilli, seeded and chopped
1 red pepper, halved and seeded	1 teaspoon ground ginger
100 g (4 oz) broccoli	200 ml (7 fl oz) coconut cream
4 tablespoons sunflower oil	Juice of 1 lime
1 tablespoon white-wine vinegar	225 g (8 oz) soft Chinese-style noodles
1 teaspoon sesame oil	Sunflower oil for deep-frying
1 teaspoon plus 1 tablespoon soy sauce	Salt and freshly ground black pepper
1 tablespoon sesame seeds	Chopped fresh mint and coriander, to garnish

Cut two carrots, two spring onions, half the red pepper and half of the stalk of the broccoli into thin matchsticks. Mix 2 tablespoons of the sunflower oil, the vinegar, sesame oil, the teaspoon of soy sauce and salt and pepper to taste. Put the mixed vegetable strips in a bowl, add the dressing and toss together. Dry-fry the sesame seeds in a small frying-pan for 1–2 minutes, until golden; then set aside.

Diagonally slice the remaining carrots. Chop the rest of the red pepper and slice the rest of the stalk of the broccoli. Cut the rest of the broccoli into small florets. Heat a tablespoon of sunflower oil in a wok, add the sliced carrots, broccoli stalks and florets, red pepper, green beans, garlic and chilli and stir-fry for 3 minutes. Add the ginger and cook for a minute. Add the tablespoon of soy sauce, the coconut cream and lime juice and cook for 3 minutes more.

Heat the oil to 190°C (375°F). Then add a quarter of the noodles and deep-fry them for 30 seconds, until crisp. Drain on absorbent kitchen paper.

Diagonally slice the remaining two spring onions. Heat a tablespoon of sunflower oil in a wok, add the spring onions and cook for a minute. Add the rest of the noodles and cook for 2 minutes.

To serve, pile the spring onions and noodles on a serving plate and spoon over the stir-fried vegetables. Arrange the deep-fried noodles on top of the mixed vegetable salad. Sprinkle the toasted sesame seeds and chopped mint and coriander over the stir-fry and the salad, to garnish.

READY STEADY COOK Tips

• *If you don't have a thermometer or a deep-fryer, check that the oil is hot enough for deep-frying the noodles by throwing in a cube of day-old bread: it should brown in 30 seconds.*

• *One way to perfect stir-fries, as always, is to cut the vegetables into pieces that are roughly the same size, so they cook in about the same time.*

• *Precise cooking times and attention to what's happening in the wok are vital for all kinds of stir-frying. Make sure you prepare as much as possible before you begin cooking, so you can give the cooking your full attention.*

RICHARD CAWLEY

HAVE YOURSELF A VEGGIE LITTLE CHRISTMAS

Chestnut and cranberry pudding and orange salad, with garlic mushrooms on toast

Harriet Olaleye, from London, wanted a new idea for a vegetarian Christmas dinner, using the traditional Christmas ingredients of chestnuts and cranberries. Richard obliged with this traditional-style suet pudding.

SERVES 2 UNACCOMPANIED AND 4 WITH EXTRA VEGETABLES

FOR THE PUDDING
225 g (8 oz) self-raising flour
100 g (4 oz) vegetable suet
½ teaspoon dried oregano
2 tablespoons sunflower oil
1 large onion, chopped
240 g (8½ oz) tin of peeled chestnuts, roughly chopped
1 dessert apple, peeled, cored and chopped
225 g (8 oz) fresh or defrosted frozen cranberries
1 tablespoon chopped fresh sage
75 ml (3 fl oz) red wine
50 ml (2 fl oz) water
Salt and freshly ground black pepper

FOR THE GARLIC MUSHROOMS
25 g (1 oz) butter
1 tablespoon olive oil
225 g (8 oz) button mushrooms, quartered
2 garlic cloves, crushed
150 ml (5 fl oz) double cream
1 tablespoon chopped fresh parsley
4 slices of bread

FOR THE ORANGE SALAD
1 teaspoon lemon juice
1 tablespoon olive oil
2 tablespoons snipped fresh chives
2 oranges, peeled and segmented
Snipped fresh chives, to garnish

Mix the flour, suet, oregano and seasoning in a bowl. Stir in enough cold water, a little at a time, to make a smooth, firm dough. Turn out on to a lightly floured surface, knead gently and roll out to a circle measuring about 30 cm (12 in) in diameter and 5 mm (¼ in) thick. Cut out one quarter of the circle and set it aside for the lid. Use the remaining three-quarters of the pastry to line an oiled 1.2 litre (2 pint) pudding basin or microwave-proof glass bowl. Bring the cut edges together to form a cone shape. Press the join together.

Heat 2 tablespoons of oil in a pan, add the onion and cook for 5 minutes, stirring occasionally. Put two-thirds of the onion in a bowl, with the chestnuts, apple, half of the cranberries, the sage and seasoning; mix well. Spoon into the pastry case and pour in the wine and water. Roll the reserved piece of pastry to make a lid for the pudding. Brush the edge of the lid with water, put the pastry lid on and smooth the seam to seal the pudding; trim the top edges. Cover with cling film and cook in the microwave on full power for 10 minutes.

For the garlic mushrooms, melt the butter and olive oil in a frying-pan, add the button mushrooms and cook for 3 minutes. Add the garlic, half of the reserved onion, the rest of the cranberries, the cream, parsley and seasoning and cook for 2 minutes. Toast the slices of bread, until golden.

To make the orange salad, mix the lemon juice, oil, chives and seasoning. Add the orange segments and the rest of the onion and toss together.

To serve, spoon the garlic mushrooms over the toast and garnish with fresh chives. Serve the chestnut and cranberry pudding with the orange salad.

READY STEADY COOK Tip

• *You can still have Chirstmas dinner with a traditional feel, even though it is vegetarian, if you use the classic Christmas ingredients (except the turkey) in imaginative ways. Consider making chestnut or sage and onion stuffing balls and serving little vegetarian sausages, for example.*

RAQUEL'S RAVISHING MUSHROOM TART

Raquel Addleman, from Bury, Lancashire, is one of twins. She and her sister wear the same clothes and live in the same road and their babies were born within hours of each other. Raquel had never cooked with filo pastry and sun-dried tomatoes, so she asked Richard to show her how to use them to advantage.

SERVES 2

25 g (1 oz) butter, melted	Juice of ½ lemon
5 sheets of filo pastry, halved	1 tablespoon French mustard
2 eggs	5 sun-dried tomato halves in oil, sliced
1 tablespoon olive oil	1 teaspoon caster sugar
100 g (4 oz) mushrooms, sliced	½ frisée lettuce
2 garlic cloves, chopped	Salt and freshly ground black pepper
3 tablespoons chopped fresh parsley	1 tablespoon grated parmesan, to serve

Pre-heat the oven to gas mark 6, 200°C (400°F). Butter two 10 cm (4 in) round flan cases or tartlet tins and line each with 4–5 layers of filo, brushing each layer with melted butter. Trim the edges. Place the pastry cases on a baking sheet and bake in the preheated oven for 8–10 minutes.

To poach the eggs, firstly, fill a bowl with boiling water. Put the two raw eggs (still in their shells) in the bowl and leave for 60 seconds. Remove the eggs and break them into a pan of boiling water. Cook the eggs for 2–3 minutes; they should stay in perfect shape. (You can cook the eggs ahead of time and keep them in a bowl of cold water. To reheat them, return them to boiling water for a minute.)

Sauté the mushrooms in the olive oil. Season and add half the garlic. Cook for 5 minutes. Then add the parsley and cook for a further 2 minutes.

To make the salad dressing, mix together 2 tablespoons of oil from the sun-dried tomatoes (or olive oil), the lemon juice, mustard, the remaining garlic, the sun-dried tomatoes and caster sugar. Toss the lettuce in the dressing.

To serve, spoon the mushrooms into the filo pastry cases and top each with a poached egg. Sprinkle the parmesan on top and serve with the salad.

P A T R I C K   A N T H O N Y

DANIELLE'S CAULIFLOWER CHARMER

Cauliflower and root vegetables in a creamy curry sauce

A health-conscious student of dance and drama, Danielle Campbell-Scott brought along her favourite vegetarian ingredients. Patrick concocted a delicious curry: root vegetables take wonderfully well to being cooked with spices, because they absorb the flavours beautifully. Serve this with plain boiled rice for a vegetarian main course.

SERVES 2

350 g (12 oz) sweet potato, peeled and cubed
1 potato, peeled and cubed
1 teaspoon paprika
½ cauliflower, cut in florets
1 tablespoon sunflower oil
25 g (1 oz) butter
½ onion, finely chopped
½ fresh green chilli, seeded and finely chopped
1 teaspoon ground turmeric
1 teaspoon garam masala
1 teaspoon ground coriander
1 teaspoon ground cumin
½ green pepper, seeded and chopped
2 tablespoons natural yoghurt
1 egg yolk

TO SERVE
1 banana, sliced
Lemon juice
Sprigs of coriander or parsley (optional), to garnish

Cook the sweet potato and potato in lightly salted, boiling water for 15 minutes. Drain them and sprinkle over the paprika. Meanwhile, steam the cauliflower for 10 minutes.

For the curry sauce, heat the oil and butter, fry the onion and chilli for 2–3 minutes until softened. Add the turmeric, garam masala, coriander, cumin and 6 tablespoons of water. Season and cook for 5 minutes. Add the green pepper and cook for a further 10 minutes.

Meanwhile, mix the yoghurt and egg yolk together in a small bowl. (The yolk will stop the yoghurt from curdling when it is cooked.) Stir the yoghurt and egg mix into the curry sauce and continue to cook the sauce for 3 minutes.

Slice the banana and squeeze some lemon juice over it, to stop it from discolouring.

To serve, place the cauliflower in the centre of a plate and surround it with the potatoes. Pour over the curry sauce and garnish with coriander or parsley, if you like. Serve the banana slices as an accompaniment.

READY STEADY COOK Tips

• *Make sure the sauce doesn't boil after you add the yoghurt and egg yolk mixture: although the egg yolk will stop the yoghurt from curdling, if the heat is too high the yolk will go grainy.*

• *Other kinds of fruit can be served as a refreshing accompaniment to all kinds of curries and spicy dishes. Even ordinary sliced apples and oranges, perhaps with a few raisins and a little desiccated coconut, can make a meal more special, or splash out on more exotic tropical fruit like mangoes.*

PATRICK ANTHONY

BARBARA'S FILO DREAMBOATS

Filo pastry 'boats' with two vegetable fillings

Patrick was asked to create a really delectable vegetarian idea by Barbara Roll, from Abridge, Essex, who wants to avoid eating red meat and fish. Half the filo containers are filled with a delicious and fragrant mixture of chestnut mushrooms and aubergines; the others with a rich and piquant courgette and tomato filling.

SERVES 2
25 g (1 oz) butter, melted
6 sheets of filo pastry

FOR THE AUBERGINE FILLING
1 tablespoon sunflower oil
1 tablespoon olive oil
$\frac{1}{2}$ aubergine, cut in 1 cm ($\frac{1}{2}$ in) cubes
100 g (4 oz) chestnut mushrooms, roughly chopped
1 teaspoon lemon-grass paste

FOR THE COURGETTE FILLING
1 tablespoon sunflower oil
1 small courgette, cubed
$\frac{1}{2}$ red onion, chopped

3 tomatoes, skinned and chopped
1 teaspoon caster sugar
1 teaspoon tomato purée
$\frac{1}{2}$ teaspoon Dijon mustard
$\frac{1}{2}$ teaspoon balsamic vinegar
Salt and freshly ground black pepper

TO SERVE
4 tablespoons double cream
A few drops of sesame oil
A few drops of Tabasco sauce
4 tablespoons Greek yoghurt
1 tablespoon chopped fresh flatleaf parsley
1 tablespoon chopped fresh basil
Sprigs of flatleaf parsley and strips of courgette skin, to garnish

Pre-heat the oven to gas mark 6, 200°C (400°F). Put four upturned ramekin dishes on a baking tray and brush them with melted butter. Cut six sheets of filo pastry in half, brush each with melted butter and layer three pieces loosely over each ramekin dish. Trim if necessary. Bake in the oven for 10–12 minutes, until golden and crisp.

Heat the sunflower and olive oils in a frying-pan, add the aubergine and mushrooms and season well with black pepper. Cook for 3 minutes, stirring occasionally. Add the lemon-grass paste and cook for another 3 minutes. For the courgette filling, heat the oil in another frying-pan, add the courgette, onion, tomatoes, sugar, tomato purée and seasoning and cook for 5 minutes, stirring occasionally. Stir in the mustard and vinegar.

Take the filo baskets off the ramekin dishes and put them on the baking tray. Spoon each of the vegetable mixtures into two baskets and drizzle a tablespoon of cream over each of the courgette baskets. Return to the oven for 3 minutes.

Drizzle a few drops of sesame oil and Tabasco sauce over one side of each serving plate and put the aubergine basket on top. Spoon the Greek yoghurt on top of the aubergine mixture. Drizzle a tablespoon of cream over the other side of each serving plate and put the courgette baskets on top. Sprinkle the chopped herbs over both baskets and garnish with sprigs of parsley and strips of courgette skin.

READY STEADY COOK Tips

• *Filo pastry dries out very quickly and becomes brittle and hard to handle. To prevent this, put the sheets you are not working with under a clean, slightly damp tea towel.*

• *This dish would also be delicious with more unusual kinds of mushrooms, such as oyster, shiitake or even fresh wild mushrooms, if you can get them.*

P A T R I C K   A N T H O N Y

MICHELLE'S MÉLANGE

Red and green gratin, with deep-fried artichoke 'crisps'

Busy vegetarian mother-of-two Michelle Wells, from Peterborough, brought along her family's favourite vegetables, with some Jerusalem artichokes, which she had never tried to cook. Patrick peeled them into ribbons and deep-fried them to make delicious home-made 'crisps' to serve as a crunchy garnish to this tasty gratin.

SERVES 4 AS A MAIN COURSE, 6 AS AN ACCOMPANIMENT
450 g (1 lb) greens, shredded
450 g (1 lb) broccoli, cut in florets
2 beef tomatoes

FOR THE CHEESE SAUCE
25 g (1 oz) butter
25 g (1 oz) plain flour
300 ml (10 fl oz) milk

100 g (4 oz) Cheddar cheese, half diced, half grated

FOR THE ARTICHOKE CRISPS
Sunflower oil, for deep-frying
225 g (8 oz) Jerusalem artichokes, peeled

TO GARNISH
1 tablespoon chopped fresh parsley
Bunches of fresh herbs (optional)

In a two-tier steamer, place the greens in the bottom section and steam for 8 minutes. Add the broccoli to the top section and steam for 6 minutes. (Or you could cook the vegetables in lightly salted, boiling water.) Drain the vegetables and place in a casserole dish.

Meanwhile, halve the tomatoes and put them under a hot grill for 5 minutes, until they are partially cooked. Remove from the grill. Remove the skins, chop the flesh and add to the vegetables.

For the all-in-one cheese sauce, put the butter, flour and milk in a pan, bring to the boil, whisking continuously and simmer for 2 minutes until thickened. Remove from the heat, add the diced cheese and mix well as the cheese melts. When smooth and blended, pour the cheese sauce over the vegetables. Sprinkle the grated cheese over and put the dish under a hot grill for 3 minutes, or until the cheese has melted and browned slightly.

Heat the oil for deep-frying in a small pan. Cut the artichokes into thin ribbons with a potato peeler. Deep-fry the ribbons of artichoke until crisp and golden brown. Drain on kitchen paper.

To serve, sprinkle the artichoke crisps on top of the vegetables and around the edge. Garnish with chopped parsley and bunches of fresh herbs, if you like.

PATRICK ANTHONY

WENDY'S WINTER WONDER

Stuffed mushrooms, with sautéed aubergine and cheese sauce

In a programme broadcast in the depth of winter's cold, Wendy Burnley, from Scarborough, asked Patrick to come up with an idea for a warming vegetarian dish that would be tasty enough to serve to her sister when she comes to visit. This delicious stuffed-mushroom recipe perfectly fits the bill.

SERVES 2 AS A MAIN COURSE,
4 AS A STARTER
4 large mushrooms, stalks removed and chopped finely
4 tablespoons olive oil, plus a little extra
100 g (4 oz) white rice
½ onion, finely chopped
1 garlic clove, chopped
4 fresh basil leaves, chopped
4 tablespoons tinned chopped tomatoes

½ aubergine, cubed
Salt and freshly ground black pepper

FOR THE CHEESE SAUCE
25 g (1 oz) butter
25 g (1 oz) plain flour
300 ml (10 fl oz) milk
60 g (2½ oz) Cheddar cheese, cubed
1 tablespoon double cream

Pre-heat the oven to gas mark 6, 200°C (400°F). Brush the mushroom caps with a little oil and put them in a lightly greased casserole dish. Bake in the oven for 12–15 minutes.

Bring some water to the boil and add salt. Add the rice and boil for 12 minutes. Drain the rice.

Heat a tablespoon of oil in a frying-pan, add the onion, garlic and basil, season and fry until softened, stirring occasionally. Add the tomatoes and the chopped mushroom stalks. Cook for a further 2 minutes. Add the cooked rice to the onion and tomato sauce, mix thoroughly and take off the heat.

Heat the remaining oil in a frying-pan, add the aubergine and stir-fry for 3–4 minutes. Season well.

Whisk together the butter, flour and milk in a pan over a low heat until smooth and well blended. When the sauce has thickened, add the cheese and double cream and continue to heat gently, whisking constantly, for 2 minutes.

To serve, put the mushrooms on a plate, spoon some of the rice filling into each, surround with the aubergine and pour the cheese sauce over the top.

READY STEADY COOK Tips

• *If you want to serve this as a vegetarian main course, just add some fresh vegetables for colour and texture: the stuffed mushrooms are substantial enough for a meal in themselves and the rice in the filling means you don't need any other carbohydrate.*

• *You could also serve the mushrooms with a well-flavoured tomato sauce, perhaps sprinkled with a little grated cheese and browned under a hot grill for a few moments.*

RICHARD CAWLEY

FRANCES'S FAST FEAST

Super-quick cheese soufflés, with chicory and avocado salad

Frances Lynch Smith, from Coventry, has been a vegetarian since she was in her early teens. She asked Richard to show her the quickest way to make soufflés that would be an instant hit at dinner parties. Richard served the rich soufflés with a refreshingly crisp salad in which slightly bitter chicory leaves are complemented by creamy avocado.

SERVES 2

FOR THE SOUFFLÉS
50 g (2 oz) butter
150 ml (5 fl oz) milk
25 g (1 oz) plain flour
2 eggs, separated
50 g (2 oz) Cheddar or Gruyère cheese, grated
2–3 drops of Tabasco sauce
½ teaspoon cayenne pepper
Salt and freshly ground black pepper
Fresh parsley sprigs, to garnish

FOR THE SALAD
1 avocado, stoned and mashed
1 tomato, chopped
2 tablespoons roughly chopped fresh coriander
½ onion, chopped
6 chicory leaves

For the soufflés: pre-heat the oven to gas mark 6, 200°C (400°F). Melt half of the butter and use it to grease two ramekins.

Make a white sauce by mixing the flour, milk and remaining butter in a pan. Bring to the boil, whisking continuously. Simmer for 2 minutes to thicken the sauce. Remove from the heat. Add the egg yolks, cheese, Tabasco, cayenne and seasoning and stir vigorously.

Whisk the egg whites until stiff. Fold a third into the cheese mixture with a metal spoon, then add the remainder. Pour the mixture into the ramekins and bake for 12–14 minutes, until well risen.

Mix the avocado, tomato, coriander and onion well and season. Separate the chicory leaves. Spoon a tablespoon of the avocado mixture on to each chicory leaf. Put the stuffed chicory leaves on a plate, in a star shape. Serve the soufflés separately, and garnish.

FISH DISHES

PATRICK ANTHONY

MANDY'S SALMON MARVEL

Seared salmon steaks with vegetables, cucumber salad
and herb mayonnaise

Mandy Lee, from Blackpool, loves fish but is married to a fish-hater. She brought salmon
steaks to the programme and wanted a really special recipe as a treat for herself.

SERVES 2

2 salmon steaks
Sunflower oil
225 g (8 oz) new potatoes, lightly scraped
1 leek, sliced in thin strips
1 carrot, grated into ribbons

FOR THE CUCUMBER SALAD
1 teaspoon Dijon mustard
1 tablespoon balsamic vinegar

3 tablespoons extra virgin olive oil
1 cucumber
Salt and freshly ground black pepper
Sprig of fresh coriander, to garnish

FOR THE HERB MAYONNAISE
4 tablespoons mayonnaise
1 tablespoon chopped fresh dill
1 tablespoon chopped fresh mint

For the salad, whisk together the mustard, seasoning, vinegar and oil.
Peel strips off the length of the cucumber, so you are left with stripes of
green. Slice the cucumber and arrange the slices in a bowl. Pour a
little of the vinaigrette over the top. Garnish with the fresh coriander.

Put the mayonnaise in a ramekin and stir in the dill and mint.

Rinse the salmon steaks, pat them dry and brush lightly with oil. Heat
in a heavy-based pan, add the steaks and sear for a minute each side.
Turn the heat down and cook the salmon gently for 6 minutes, or until
the flesh comes away cleanly from the bone.

Meanwhile, gently cook the potatoes in simmering, lightly salted
water for 10–12 minutes, or until just cooked. Blanch the leek strips
and carrot ribbons in boiling water until just tender. Drain all the
vegetables. Put the salmon steaks on warmed plates and arrange
vegetables around them. Serve with the salad and herb mayonnaise.

P A T R I C K   A N T H O N Y

RACHEL'S THAILAND TREAT

Prawns in a creamy Thai-curry sauce, with rice

Rachel Gill and her family love exotic dishes, so she produced prawns and creamed coconut and challenged Patrick to make an oriental treat.

SERVES 4
Salt
225 g (8 oz) long-grain, Thai jasmine or basmati rice, to serve
½ teaspoon ground turmeric

FOR THE SAUCE
Groundnut oil, for frying
200 g (7 oz) baby corn, halved
200 g (7 oz) mangetout
½ fresh green chilli, seeded and cut in thin strips
2.5 cm (1 in) piece of root ginger, peeled and grated

A bunch of spring onions
1 onion, finely chopped
150 ml (5 fl oz) chicken or vegetable stock
Juice and grated zest of 1 lime
100 g (4 oz) button mushrooms, finely sliced
75 g (3 oz) creamed coconut, grated
½ teaspoon dried lemon grass
½ teaspoon Thai red or green curry paste
225 g (8 oz) cooked, peeled prawns
150 ml (5 fl oz) double cream
2 tablespoons chopped fresh coriander, to garnish

For the rice, pour ½ teaspoon of salt into a large pan of boiling water, add the rice and turmeric and boil for 12 minutes. Drain the rice, put it in a sieve over boiling water, cover it with a tea towel and leave it for 2 minutes, to fluff up.

For the sauce, heat a tablespoon of oil in a frying-pan and, when very hot, add the corn and mangetout and stir-fry them quickly until they are charred on the outside. Then add the chilli, ginger, spring onions, onion, stock, lime juice, mushrooms, creamed coconut, lemon grass and curry paste and cook for 5 minutes over a moderate heat, stirring occasionally. Next add the prawns and cook for just under

2 minutes, to heat them through. Lastly, stir in the cream and heat through for 1–2 minutes. To serve, pour the prawns and sauce on top of a bed of rice and garnish with fresh coriander and zest of lime.

PATRICK ANTHONY

JANE'S FRANCO-ORIENTAL PLAICE

Poached plaice with vegetables and creamy mushroom sauce

This recipe combines plaice fillets cooked in a French style – poached in a flavourful court-bouillon and served with a creamy mushroom sauce – with wok-sweet stir-fried vegetables for a refreshingly different oriental-style accompaniment. Jane Atkey, from Surrey, loves entertaining but had never cooked a flat fish like plaice before, so she asked Patrick to show her how.

SERVES 4

1 teaspoon soy sauce
100 g (4 oz) spinach, thoroughly washed
100 g (4 oz) mangetout
15 g (½ oz) butter

FOR THE FISH

150 ml (5 fl oz) white wine
1 tablespoon lemon juice
4 plaice fillets, skinned
Salt and freshly ground white or black pepper

FOR THE SAUCE

35 g (1½ oz) butter
¼ onion, finely chopped
150 ml (5 fl oz) double cream
4 button mushrooms, thinly sliced
Sprigs of fresh parsley, to garnish

FOR THE VEGETABLES

2 tablespoons sunflower oil
3 leeks, cut into 5 mm (¼ in) slices
225 g (8 oz) carrots, peeled and cut in batons

For the fish, heat the wine and lemon juice in a large saucepan and season with salt and pepper. Poach the plaice in this court-bouillon (stock) by first bringing the stock to boil; after 30 seconds, remove the pan from the heat, cover and leave it to stand for 3 minutes. Remove the plaice and keep it warm. Strain the bouillon and set it aside.

Heat the oil in a wok and stir-fry the leeks and carrots. When the vegetables are beginning to brown, add the soy sauce.

Put the spinach in a saucepan and cover it with a lid. Put the pan on the heat and cook the spinach in just the water clinging to the leaves for about 40 seconds, or until the leaves have begun to wilt. Drain thoroughly and keep warm.

Blanch the mangetout in a little water for about a minute. Refresh them under cold, running water. Slice them into shreds and fry them quickly in 15 g (½ oz) butter, just before serving.

For the sauce, melt the butter in a saucepan, add the onion and cook until softened. Add the reserved fish stock, the double cream, and the mushrooms and cook for 3–4 minutes, until the sauce has reduced a little.

To serve, pile a bed of spinach in the centre of a plate, lay the plaice on top, surround it with the vegetables and pour the sauce over the top. Garnish with fresh parsley sprigs.

READY STEADY COOK Tips

• *Don't be tempted to cook the fillets of plaice for any longer: the texture will not be so good and the fillets may begin to fall apart.*

• *If you have the plaice filleted and skinned for you, ask for the bones. Chop them roughly and add them to the court-bouillon for extra flavour. They will be strained out when the fish has cooked.*

PATRICK ANTHONY

SUZY'S TROUT SENSATION

Pan-fried trout with a rocket butter sauce

Trout is the favourite fish of the husband of Suzy Anthony, from Southgate, London. Suzy wanted a new way to cook trout and also ideas for cooking with rocket, which she had used in salads but not hot.

SERVES 2	3 carrots, grated
	1 large courgette, grated
FOR THE TROUT	1 tablespoon soy sauce
2 trout	2 drops of Tabasco sauce
2 tablespoons finely chopped onion	Salt and freshly ground white or black pepper
1 tablespoon chopped fresh dill	
1 tablespoon chopped fresh tarragon	**FOR THE SAUCE**
1 tablespoon chopped fresh parsley	1 egg yolk
1 teaspoon paprika	1 teaspoon Dijon mustard
1 tablespoon sunflower oil	2 teaspoons red wine vinegar
	40 g (1½ oz) butter, melted
FOR THE VEGETABLES	A few rocket leaves, shredded
1 tablespoon sunflower oil	A few parsley sprigs, to garnish (optional)

Stuff the trout with onion, dill, tarragon and parsley. Season both sides of the trout with the paprika. Pan-fry the fish in a tablespoon of sunflower oil for 8–10 minutes, turning them half-way through.

Fry the carrots and courgette in the remaining tablespoon of oil in a pre-heated wok. Add the soy sauce and Tabasco, season and cook for 3–5 minutes.

Mix the egg yolk, mustard, vinegar and salt and pepper together in a bowl. Whisk in the melted butter; then add the rocket leaves.

To serve, put the trout in the centre of a plate. Spoon courgettes and carrots around the fish and pour over the rocket sauce. Garnish with sprigs of parsley, if you like.

P A T R I C K   A N T H O N Y

DOT'S DELIGHT

Cod steak with fried potatoes and tomato toasts

Like many people, Dot Kirby, from Harleston, Norfolk, doesn't cook fish. She asked Patrick to create a delicious fish dish that was easy to do and tasty enough to tempt her into becoming a fish-eater.

SERVES 1	$\frac{1}{2}$ teaspoon ginger purée
5 tablespoons sunflower oil	$\frac{1}{2}$ teaspoon balsamic vinegar
225 g (8 oz) potatoes, peeled and cut in 2 cm	175 g (6 oz) thick cod steak
($\frac{3}{4}$ in) cubes	7.5 cm (3 in) French bread, halved lengthways
2 garlic cloves, halved	2 tomatoes, sliced
1 sprig of rosemary	$\frac{1}{4}$ teaspoon dried oregano
50 g (2 oz) piece of smoked	$\frac{1}{4}$ teaspoon dried mixed herbs
streaky bacon, cubed	Salt and freshly ground pepper
50 g (2 oz) button mushrooms, sliced	Sprigs of flatleaf parsley, to garnish

Heat 2 tablespoons of oil in a small frying-pan, add the potatoes and fry for 5 minutes. Add the garlic and rosemary to the potatoes and fry for a further 3 minutes, until the potatoes are tender and golden. Remove the garlic and rosemary.

Meanwhile, cook the bacon in a tablespoon of oil for 2 minutes; then add the mushrooms, ginger purée and vinegar and cook gently for 5 minutes, turning occasionally. Heat a tablespoon of oil in a small frying-pan and fry the cod for 5–6 minutes, turning it once.

Toast the slices of bread, cut-side up, until golden. Heat the remaining oil in a small frying-pan, add the tomatoes and sprinkle over the oregano, mixed herbs and seasoning. Cook over a high heat for 2–3 minutes.

Make a bed of potatoes in the centre of a warmed plate. Put the cod steak on top and a piece of bread on each side; arrange the tomatoes on them. Spoon the bacon mixture on top and garnish.

PATRICK ANTHONY

GARRY'S PANTOMIME PILLOWS

Puff-pastry pillows of smoked haddock, prawns and mushrooms

In memory of the time stage manager Garry Thomas, from Manchester, played the back end of a pantomime cow, Patrick christened these 'pillows' of puff pastry, filled with a delicious mixture of smoked haddock, prawns and mushrooms in a creamy sauce.

SERVES 2
Ready-rolled puff pastry, cut in
2 x 10 cm (4 in) squares
225 g (8 oz) smoked haddock fillet, skinned
450 ml (15 fl oz) chicken stock
150 ml (5 fl oz) white wine
2 spring onions
4 tablespoons double cream
75 g (3 oz) button mushrooms, chopped
75 g (3 oz) peeled prawns

FOR THE CABBAGE
25 g (1 oz) butter
1 tablespoon soft brown sugar
1 tablespoon soy sauce
4–5 drops of Tabasco sauce
2–3 tablespoons water
½ green cabbage, shredded
Sprigs of parsley, to garnish

Pre-heat the oven to gas mark 7, 220°C (425°F). Line two 10 cm (4 in) tart tins with the pastry and trim the edges (or use a well-greased baking tray). Prick the pastry bases, and bake them for 10–12 minutes. When risen and golden, turn out from the tins and cool.

Poach the fish in the stock for 7–10 minutes. When cooked, discard the stock and flake the haddock in a bowl. Keep warm.

In a frying-pan, bring the white wine to the boil. Add the spring onions and cook for a couple of minutes. Stir in the cream and mushrooms and continue to cook until the sauce reduces and thickens. Add the prawns.

Melt the butter and brown sugar in a frying-pan. Add the soy sauce, Tabasco and water. Stir in the cabbage and cook for 4–5 minutes.

Slice the puff pastry horizontally through the middle, to make a top and bottom.

To serve, place the bases of the puff pastry tarts on a plate. Divide the haddock between each base and spoon over the prawn and mushroom sauce. Then place the lid of the pastry on top. Spoon the cabbage on the side and garnish with fresh parsley.

P A T R I C K   A N T H O N Y

HEATHER'S HAPPY CRAB

Dressed crab with home-made mayonnaise

Heather Elliott, from Chesterfield, Derbyshire, used to be a competitive body-builder but is now at home with a young baby. She loves seafood and asked Patrick to show her how to dress a crab. It's well worth making home-made mayonnaise to serve with a fresh crab — simple but delicious.

SERVES 4	65 ml (2½ fl oz) sunflower oil
2 slices of white bread, crusts removed	65 ml (2½ fl oz) olive oil
1 cooked crab, shell-on,	Salt and freshly ground black pepper
weighing 700 g (1½ lb)	½ lettuce, shredded, to serve
3 teaspoons white wine vinegar	
2 eggs	**TO GARNISH**
1 egg yolk	Parsley sprigs
1 teaspoon Dijon mustard	1 lemon, quartered

Make the bread into breadcrumbs.

To dress the crab, twist off the claws and legs. Press down on the mouth end of the crab to split the body apart. Remove and discard the 'dead man's fingers' (part of the stomach, located under the shell). Spoon the brown flesh into a bowl, add salt and pepper, a teaspoon of vinegar and the breadcrumbs. Wash the crab shell, pat it dry, and reserve it.

Crack open the claws and legs with a rolling pin and remove the white flesh. Put it in a separate bowl and set it to one side.

Hard-boil the eggs, piercing a pinhole in the wide end to stop the shell from cracking. When cooked, shell and chop the eggs.

To make the mayonnaise, whisk together the egg yolk, mustard and the remaining 2 teaspoons of vinegar. Add the oil very slowly, whisking vigorously and continuously, until thick. Spoon a little of the mayonnaise over the white crab meat and mash together.

To serve, put the brown flesh into the crab shell and spoon the white meat on top of the brown. On a plate, make a bed of lettuce and arrange the dressed crab on top. Garnish with the chopped egg, parsley and lemon. Serve the rest of the mayonnaise separately.

READY STEADY COOK Tips

• *To stop the mayonnaise from separating, add the oil a drop at a time to start with. When you've added about half the oil, you can pour it in in a slow, steady stream.*

• *If the worst happens and the mayonnaise curdles, don't despair! Start again with a fresh egg yolk and whisk the curdled mixture into it a drop at a time.*

Above: Rachel's Delectable Thai Dream (page 10).
Below: Pork and Cider with Ros (page 71).

Above: Garry's Pantomime Pillows (page 30).
Below: Claire's Turkish Creation (page 75).

Above: Ruth's Hoki-coki (page 36).
Below: Sandra's Chilli Sensation (page 59).

Above: Easter Strawberry Nests (page 88).
Below: Terry's Orient Express (page 44).

Above: Mandy's Salmon Marvel (page 24).
Below: Rachel's Ravishing Mushroom Tart (page 14).

Above: Geraldine's Eastern Promise (page 46).
Below: Steak Mother Abbess (page 64).

Above: Dot's Delight (page 29).
Below: Vicky's Pineapple Victory (page 84).

Above: Sarah's Steak Sensation (page 76).
Below: Couscous with Spatchcocked Quail (page 51).

R I C H A R D   C A W L E Y

YULE DROOL BREAKFAST

Kedgeree, savoury croissants and scrambled eggs

This is a triple-decker breakfast spread of kedgeree, ham and cheese croissants and herby scrambled eggs. Jacqueline Walker was expecting her in-laws to join her and her family for Christmas in Fife, Scotland, and she wanted to impress them with a really special Boxing Day breakfast.

SERVES 2

FOR THE KEDGEREE
50 g (2 oz) white rice, rinsed thoroughly
1 small kipper fillet, skinned
1 small smoked haddock fillet, skinned
15 g ($\frac{1}{2}$ oz) butter
$\frac{1}{4}$ onion, chopped
$\frac{1}{2}$ teaspoon, garam masala
1 hard-boiled egg, chopped roughly

FOR THE CROISSANTS
2 croissants
2 slices of ham
50 g (2 oz) Edam cheese, grated

FOR THE HERBY SCRAMBLED EGGS
4 eggs
2 tablespoons double cream
25 g (1 oz) butter
2 tablespoons chopped fresh dill
1 tablespoon chopped fresh parsley
Salt and freshly ground black pepper

Pre-heat the oven to gas mark 6, 200°C (400°F). Bring a pan of water to the boil and cook the rice for about 8–10 minutes. Drain the rice, return it to the pan and set it to one side.

Put the kipper and haddock fillets on some lightly buttered foil and loosely wrap them up. Put the parcel on a baking tray in the oven for 7–8 minutes. Remove and flake the fish.

Meanwhile, melt 15 g ($\frac{1}{2}$ oz) of butter in a saucepan, add the onion and cook until soft. Stir in the garam masala. Add the flaked fish, hard-boiled egg and rice and mix well but gently.

Slice open the croissants, and fill them with ham and cheese. Put the croissants in an ovenproof dish and bake for about 6–8 minutes.

To make the herby scrambled eggs, break the eggs into a bowl and whisk lightly together with the cream. Melt the butter in a saucepan, add the egg mixture, the dill and parsley, season and stir continuously over a low heat until scrambled.

To serve, spoon some of the scrambled egg and kedgeree (heat through before serving) on to each plate and accompany with the filled croissants.

RICHARD CAWLEY

LITTLE FISHES IN A BASKET

Pancake baskets with seafood sauce

Scots-born Sylvia Gray, from Tyne and Wear, loves all kinds of fish – especially from the River Tyne, which runs through her home town. Richard served them in pancake baskets, in honour of Shrove Tuesday, when the programme was broadcast.

SERVES 4

FOR THE PANCAKES
150g (6 oz) plain flour, sifted
3 eggs
450 ml (15 fl oz) milk
Sunflower oil for frying
Salt and freshly ground black pepper

FOR THE FILLING
2 red onions, thinly sliced
2 garlic cloves, crushed
400 g (14 oz) tin of tomatoes
1 tablespoon chopped fresh parsley
150 g (6 oz) packet of mixed seafood
150 g (6 oz) packet of crabsticks, chopped
3 tablespoons red wine vinegar
5 tablespoons caster sugar
1 large handful of spinach, thoroughly washed

Pre-heat the oven to gas mark 6, 200°C (400°F). Grease the outside of four ramekins and put them, upside-down, on a baking sheet.

To make the pancake batter, blend the flour, eggs and pinch of salt to a smooth batter. Slowly add the milk and continue to blend until thoroughly mixed.

Heat a little oil in a frying-pan. When it is very hot, pour in a little of the batter, tilting the pan to ensure that the whole base is covered; the pancake should be fairly thick. Make four pancakes of this size. Put a pancake over each upturned ramekin and bake on the middle shelf for 12–14 minutes, or until crisp. Allow the pancakes to cool, then remove the ramekins and turn the pancake baskets over.

Make six more, slightly thinner, pancakes. Stack and slice them so that they resemble tagliatelle. These can be served later as a dessert with lemon and sugar.

For the sauce, fry half a red onion in a tablespoon of oil until soft, covered. Add the garlic and tomatoes and simmer for 5 minutes. Stir in the parsley and continue to simmer. After 5 minutes, add the seafood and crabsticks. Season and cook for a further 2 minutes.

To make the sweet pickled onions, heat the vinegar and sugar together. When the sugar has dissolved, remove from the heat and pour over the remaining onions. Leave for 3–4 minutes; then drain.

To serve, place the spinach leaves around the outside of a large plate. Sprinkle the pickled onions over the spinach. Place the pancake baskets in the centre and fill them with the seafood sauce.

READY STEADY COOK Tips

• *If you don't have the seafood and crabsticks, use prawns and or cubes of white fish, or even flaked canned tuna.*

• *For a vegetarian version, replace the seafood with cubes of tofu or perhaps a fairly firm-textured vegetable such as aubergine.*

RICHARD CAWLEY

RUTH'S HOKI-COKI

Baked fish with carrot and orange salad

Ruth Nelhams, from Kidderminster, loves fishing and it was during her hours spent on the riverbank that she met her future husband. Richard Cawley showed her how to cook New Zealand hoki, a delicious inexpensive white fish, similar to cod in taste and texture, in a paper parcel: 'en papillote'.

SERVES 2	2 tablespoons double cream
1 green pepper, halved and seeded	Salt and freshly ground black pepper
1 tablespoon olive oil	
¼ onion, finely chopped	**FOR THE SALAD**
1 large hoki fillet, halved, or 2 small	4 carrots, peeled and grated
fillets	1 orange, peeled and segmented
1 tomato, chopped	1 teaspoon balsamic vinegar
1 tablespoon chopped fresh parsley	Juice of ½ lemon
Juice of ½ lemon	4 tablespoons olive oil

Pre-heat the oven to gas mark 6, 200°C (400°F). Chop half the pepper finely and cut the rest in thin strips.

Fry the onion and the chopped pepper in the oil. Season and cook for 8 minutes.

Take a large sheet of greaseproof paper and fold it in half. Cut out two large ovals. On to each piece of paper put a piece of hoki fillet. Spoon 2–3 tablespoons of the pepper and onion mixture and a tablespoon of tomatoes on top of each fish. Season with salt and pepper, and add a sprinkle of parsley, a squeeze of lemon juice and a tablespoon of double cream. Seal the papillote by folding over the edge of the paper, leaving a pocket of air over the fish. Put the fish parcels in an ovenproof dish and bake in the preheated oven for about 10 minutes.

For the salad, mix the carrots and orange segments in a bowl.
Whisk together the vinegar, lemon juice and oil. Season to taste. Pour
the vinaigrette over the carrot and orange salad and spoon the salad
on to a plate. Decorate with strips of green pepper. Put a papillote on
each plate and serve immediately; each diner opens his or her own
parcel at the table, releasing the delicious cooking aroma.

READY STEADY COOK Tips

• *Cooking 'en papillote' is a really good, healthy way to cook all
kinds of fish fillets, such as salmon steaks or cutlets. It also works
for boneless, skinless chicken breasts and turkey steaks. Vary the
aromatics that you add, according to the main ingredient, for
example, a little lemon juice, white wine, garlic and chopped fresh
herbs for chicken. Adjust the cooking times accordingly.*

• *If your courage fails you and you want to make sure that the fish
is cooked before you serve it, just open the parcels and dish them
up in the kitchen.*

RICHARD CAWLEY

RISING-STAR FISH WITH VEGETABLES

Jennie Eriksen, from Broxbourne, Hertfordshire, brought along some of her Norwegian husband's favourite ingredients and begged for some new ideas for transforming them into a meal to satisfy her six-foot-four husband's huge appetite.

SERVES 2

½ aubergine, cut in 5 mm (¼ in) slices
1 tablespoon olive oil

FOR THE VEGETABLES
3 tablespoons olive oil
225 g (8 oz) potatoes, cut in 1 cm (½ in) cubes
2 garlic cloves, crushed
1 onion, chopped
1 courgette, cubed
2 tomatoes, chopped

1 teaspoon dried mixed herbs
100 ml (4 fl oz) white wine
1 tablespoon chopped fresh parsley
2 teaspoons tomato purée
Salt and freshly ground black pepper

FOR THE FISH
50 g (2 oz) butter
350 g (12 oz) huss (dogfish)
2 tablespoons plain flour, seasoned
Sprigs of flatleaf parsley, to garnish

Pre-heat the oven to gas mark 5, 190°C (375°F). Put the aubergine slices on a lightly oiled baking sheet and brush them very lightly with oil. Roast in the oven for 15 minutes.

Meanwhile, heat 2 tablespoons of oil in a frying-pan, add the potatoes and seasoning and cook for 5 minutes, turning occasionally. Stir in a crushed garlic clove and cook for a further 3–4 minutes, until the potatoes are tender and golden.

Heat the last tablespoon of oil in a frying-pan, add the onion and cook for 3 minutes. Stir in the courgette and the other crushed garlic clove and cook for 3 minutes. Add the tomatoes, mixed herbs, wine, parsley, tomato purée and seasoning and cook for 5 minutes.

Clarify the butter by melting it in a small pan over a gentle heat, spooning off any white foam which comes to the surface. Then carefully pour off the clear golden liquid, leaving any sediment at the bottom of the pan. Cut the fish into two equal pieces and remove the backbone by cutting either side with a sharp knife, but not cutting right through. Carefully cut out the bone and lie the flesh flat. Coat the pieces in the seasoned flour and shake off the excess. Heat 2 tablespoons of clarified butter in a frying-pan, add the fish and cook it for 6–8 minutes, turning once, until lightly browned.

To serve, put four slices of roasted aubergine on each serving plate. Place the fish on top and spoon the potatoes and courgette mixture around the edge. Garnish with a sprig of flatleaf parsley.

READY STEADY COOK Tips

• *Clarifying the butter is really worthwhile, because it allows you to heat the butter high enough for a good frying temperature, without the risk of the milky residue burning. Clarified butter keeps well in the refrigerator.*

• *Roasting vegetables in the oven gives them a wonderfully sweet flavour and a delicious skin. Branch out from the usual potatoes and parsnips: try aubergines, as here, cloves of garlic, halved peppers, tomatoes, leeks, celery, courgettes and other squashes. The choice is almost limitless and it's such an easy, no-fuss way of serving a wider than usual variety of vegetables.*

POULTRY AND GAME

RICHARD CAWLEY

TURKEY ESCALOPES WITH BEURRE BLANC SAUCE

Married, with seven children and another on the way, Janet Meredith from Manchester was hoping for a new idea for serving ever-popular poultry. This marinated turkey recipe has lots of flavour and is ready in next to no time.

SERVES 4	FOR THE BEURRE BLANC SAUCE
150 ml (5 fl oz) white wine	300 ml (10 fl oz) chicken stock
3 tablespoons soy sauce	2 tablespoons white wine
1 tablespoon cornflour, blended with	2.5 cm (1 in) root ginger, peeled and chopped
a little cold water	2 spring onions, roughly chopped
4 turkey escalopes	1 tablespoon soy sauce
1 broccoli, cut in florets	75 g (3 oz) butter, cubed
1 cauliflower, cut in florets	Chopped fresh parsley and coriander,
½ head of Chinese leaves, sliced	to garnish
Olive oil, for shallow-frying	

To make the marinade, mix the white wine, soy sauce and cornflour. Add the turkey and chill for up to an hour.

Steam the broccoli and cauliflower in 1 cm of hot salted water in a large covered pan for 4–5 minutes, shaking the pan occasionally. Add the Chinese leaves and cook for 2 minutes more.

Remove the escalopes from the marinade and let them drain briefly. Pat them dry. Heat the oil in a frying-pan and fry the escalopes for 5–6 minutes on each side. Discard the marinade. You can cut the meat into strips to reduce the cooking time to 4–5 minutes.

For the sauce, put all the ingredients, except the butter, in a pan and reduce by two-thirds. Strain out the ginger and spring onions. Whisk in the cubes of cold butter over a low heat; do not allow to boil. Put the escalopes on warmed plates, pour over the sauce and garnish with chopped parsley and coriander.

RICHARD CAWLEY

DEBBIE'S LEMON CHICKEN

This is a delicious Chinese-style dish with a lemony sauce, easily made without resorting to jars of ready-made Chinese sauces. Debbie Courtney, from Epsom, Surrey, is a busy mum and self-confessed hopeless cook who relies on packet mixes and jars. She wanted Richard to show her a tasty meal prepared from fresh ingredients.

SERVES 2

FOR THE CHICKEN
75 g (3 oz) plain flour
½ teaspoon bicarbonate of soda
150 ml (5 fl oz) water
1 tablespoon white wine vinegar
Sunflower oil, for deep-frying
4 boneless, skinless chicken thighs, cut in small pieces

FOR THE SAUCE
3–4 shallots, chopped
1 tablespoon olive oil
150 ml (5 fl oz) white wine
1 heaped teaspoon cornflour
Juice of 1 lemon
1 teaspoon honey

FOR THE POTATO SALAD
450 g (1 lb) potatoes, scrubbed and cut in chunks
2 tablespoons olive oil
A squeeze of lemon juice
½ tablespoon white wine vinegar

FOR THE COLESLAW
1 tablespoon Greek yoghurt
1 tablespoon mayonnaise
½ teaspoon Dijon mustard
100 g (4 oz) coleslaw mix
1 green pepper, seeded and thinly sliced
Salt and freshly ground black pepper

TO GARNISH
Lemon wedges
1 tomato, quartered

For the deep-fried chicken, make a batter by mixing together the flour, bicarbonate of soda, water and the wine vinegar. Heat the oil until it's very hot. Dip the chicken pieces in the batter and deep-fry them for 4 minutes, until golden brown. Drain on absorbent kitchen paper.

To make the lemon sauce, sauté the shallots in the oil for 2 minutes. Add the wine and simmer for 3 minutes. Meanwhile, mix together the cornflour, lemon juice and a little water, to form a runny paste. Add this to the shallots, bring to the boil and allow the sauce to thicken. Stir in the honey and cook for a further minute.

For the potato salad, boil the potato cubes in water for 12–15 minutes. Drain the potatoes and pour over the olive oil, lemon juice and vinegar. Season and toss the potatoes.

To make the coleslaw dressing, mix together the yoghurt, mayonnaise, mustard and salt and pepper. Pour over the coleslaw and green pepper and mix thoroughly.

To serve, arrange the chicken pieces on a plate, accompanied by the lemon sauce and the warm potato salad. Garnish with lemon wedges and tomato quarters. Serve the coleslaw separately.

READY STEADY COOK Tips

• *For a simpler, yet delicious, supper, still with the Chinese theme, just serve the chicken with the lemon sauce and some plain boiled rice.*

• *Turkey steaks or boneless, tender pork, cut in strips, could be treated in the same way and would go very well with the lemon and honey sauce. Vegetarians could try cubes of tofu.*

RICHARD CAWLEY

TERRY'S ORIENT EXPRESS

Chicken in ginger and pineapple sauce, with pineapple slices and ginger pancakes

Richard thought up this idea for a home-made oriental banquet for the ingredients brought along by Terry Gould, a lover of Chinese food, from Nottingham.

SERVES 2

4 chicken thighs
3 tablespoons soy sauce
Sunflower oil, for frying
150 ml (5 fl oz) white wine

FOR THE SAUCE
½ onion, finely chopped
½ green pepper, seeded and finely chopped
1 celery stick, chopped
1 teaspoon root ginger, grated
1 garlic clove, crushed

200 g (7 oz) tin of pineapple in natural juice
Juice of 1 lime
75 ml (3 fl oz) white wine

FOR THE PANCAKES
100 g (4 oz) plain flour
1 heaped teaspoon baking powder
½ teaspoon grated root ginger
1 egg, beaten
135 ml (4½ fl oz) milk
Salt and freshly ground black pepper

Marinate the chicken in the soy sauce, ideally for at least 30 minutes. Remove the chicken, reserving the marinade, and pat it dry.

Heat 2 tablespoons of oil in a frying-pan. Fry the chicken skin-side down first. Once the skin is brown, cook the other side for a couple of minutes. Add the wine. Bring to the boil, cover and simmer for 10–12 minutes, until the chicken is cooked.

Meanwhile, in a different pan, heat another 2 tablespoons of oil and sauté the chopped onion, pepper and celery. Add the ginger, garlic, pineapple juice, lime juice and white wine. Season and simmer for 10 minutes.

Fry the pineapple slices in hot oil until golden brown.

For the pancakes, put the flour, baking powder, a pinch of salt and the reserved soy sauce in a bowl. Mix well and then add the ginger and beaten egg. Mix thoroughly whilst adding the milk and continue to beat until the mixture has a thick consistency.

Heat another 2 tablespoons of oil in a frying-pan and, when very hot, tip 3 tablespoons of the batter for each pancake into the pan, tilt the pan to spread the batter out to 10–12 cm (4–5 inches), and fry until lightly browned each side. The pancakes should be thick and puffy. Make another three pancakes in this way.

To serve, put the chicken on a plate and spoon the sauce over it. Place the ginger pancakes on the side and put a pineapple slice on top of each pancake.

READY STEADY COOK Tips

• *Marinating in soy sauce is an easy way to add delicious savoury flavours to relatively mild-flavoured meat, such as chicken, turkey or pork. You could make a vegetarian version of this dish using tofu.*

• *The ginger pancakes would be good as a dessert topped with a good syrupy sauce or fruit. As with this recipe, you can use pineapple or you can accompany them with poached pears, which go very well with ginger.*

RICHARD CAWLEY

GERALDINE'S EASTERN PROMISE

Thai chicken curry, with lemon rice and sesame beans

Geraldine Corbett, from Haslington, near Crewe, loves curries and oriental spices, but isn't very confident about cooking with them. She brought in some chicken and typical Thai flavourings and asked Richard to show her how to make a Thai-style curry from them.

SERVES 2

FOR THE RICE
175 g (6 oz) Thai fragrant rice
½ teaspoon ground turmeric
Grated zest of 2 lemons and juice
of ½ a lemon

FOR THE CHICKEN
1 tablespoon sunflower oil
1 small onion, chopped
350 g (12 oz) boneless, skinless chicken thighs
cut in 2.5 cm (1 in) chunks
2 garlic cloves, finely chopped

2.5 cm (1 in) piece root ginger, finely chopped
1 teaspoon lemon-grass paste
Tabasco sauce
200 ml (7 fl oz) coconut milk

FOR THE BEANS
1 tablespoon sesame seeds
1 teaspoon demerara sugar
1 tablespoon soy sauce
Juice of ½ a lime
Tabasco sauce
225 g (8 oz) green beans, cut in
5 cm (2 in) lengths
Sprigs of fresh coriander, to garnish

Cook the rice in a pan of boiling water, with the turmeric and lemon zest and juice for 8–10 minutes, until tender.

Meanwhile, heat the oil, add the onion and cook for a minute. Add the chicken, garlic and ginger and cook for 2 minutes. Stir in the lemon-grass paste and a few drops of Tabasco sauce and cook for 2 minutes. Add the coconut milk and simmer for 8–10 minutes, stirring now and again.

Dry-fry the sesame seeds in a small frying-pan for 3 minutes, until golden. In a pestle and mortar, grind them to a coarse paste. Add the sugar, soy sauce, lime juice and a few drops of Tabasco sauce and mix well.

Cook the beans in a pan of boiling water for 3 minutes. Drain well and toss in the sesame dressing.

To serve, spoon the rice, coconut chicken and sesame beans on to serving plates and garnish with fresh coriander.

READY STEADY COOK Tips

• *If you can't find Thai fragrant rice, substitute basmati rice.*

• *If you have a nearby Oriental food shop and can buy fresh lime leaves, adding a couple of them to the coconut sauce will enhance the fragrant lemony flavour of the lemon-grass, for a really authentic Thai flavour.*

• *Leftover coconut milk can be added to other curries and stir-fries to make them deliciously creamy and add a subtle coconut flavour to the blend of spices. Or use it instead of cream with sliced tropical fruit or for unusual and exotic milkshakes.*

RICHARD CAWLEY

EMMA AND ANNA'S CHICKEN AND PASTA DINNER

Breadcrumbed chicken with creamy pasta sauce

The family of Kirstin Whybrow, from Hatfield, Hertfordshire, love pasta, chicken and anything with a sauce. She wanted Richard to show her how to make a pasta sauce without any lumps, using spinach. Richard came up with this idea for breadcrumbed chicken, served with carrots and leeks and accompanied by pasta with a creamy leek and spinach sauce.

SERVES 2

175 g (6 oz) fusilli, bucati lunghi or spaghetti	2 carrots, cut in fine matchsticks
225 g (8 oz) boneless, skinless chicken breast	2 leeks, cut in fine matchsticks
2 tablespoons plain flour, seasoned	1 garlic clove, crushed
1 egg, beaten	150 ml (5 fl oz) double cream
50 g (2 oz) breadcrumbs	225 g (8 oz) spinach, washed and trimmed
3 tablespoons olive oil	Juice of $\frac{1}{2}$ an orange
45 g (1$\frac{3}{4}$ oz) butter	Salt and freshly ground black pepper
	Sprigs of flatleaf parsley, to garnish

Cook the pasta in a pan of boiling, salted water for 8–10 minutes until just tender. Drain.

Meanwhile, wrap the chicken loosely in cling film and bash it with a rolling pin until it's 5 mm ($\frac{1}{4}$ in) thick. Cut the chicken in half, if you like. Coat it in the flour, dip it in the egg and coat it with the breadcrumbs. Heat a tablespoon of oil and 15 g ($\frac{1}{2}$ oz) of the butter in a frying-pan, add the chicken and cook it over a moderate heat for 8 minutes, until cooked through and golden, turning once.

Heat another tablespoon of oil and 15 g ($\frac{1}{2}$ oz) of butter in a pan, add the carrots and half of the leeks and cook them gently for 8 minutes.

Heat the final tablespoon of oil and 15 g (½ oz) of butter in another pan, add the rest of the leeks and then cook them gently for 2 minutes. Add the garlic and cook for a minute. Stir in the cream and seasoning and leave to simmer for 3 minutes. Add the spinach and cook for another 3 minutes. Stir the orange juice and seasoning into the pan of carrots and leek. Then stir the pasta into the cream and spinach sauce and cook for a minute to reheat the pasta; spoon into a serving bowl.

Divide the chicken in two, if necessary, put the chicken on warmed serving plates, with the carrots and leeks, and garnish with sprigs of flatleaf parsley.

RICHARD CAWLEY

TURKEY BALLS WITH RICE

Becky Thould is from Evesham, Worcester, but is a student at Swansea University, where she is studying sociology and anthropology. Like students everywhere, Becky is on a tight budget and she asked Richard to cook her a luxury meal at an affordable price. Richard obliged with this idea for minced turkey in a creamy sauce, served with slightly spiced carrots and leeks, tomato rice and a crisp, refreshing carrot salad.

SERVES 4

225 g (8 oz) long-grain rice
400 g (14 oz) tin of chopped tomatoes, drained, juice reserved
2 garlic cloves
1 tablespoon chopped fresh flatleaf parsley
1 tablespoon chopped fresh basil
450 g (1 lb) minced turkey
100 g (4 oz) fresh breadcrumbs

1 egg
4 tablespoons olive oil
2 leeks, sliced
3 carrots
A pinch of garam masala
150 ml (5 fl oz) double cream
1 tablespoon tomato purée
Salt and freshly ground black pepper

Put the rice in a pan, with the juice from the tomatoes. Top up with water to come 1 cm ($\frac{1}{2}$ in) above the rice; then add the tomato flesh, 1 finely chopped garlic clove and seasoning. Simmer for 5 minutes. Then add the parsley and basil and simmer for another 5 minutes, until the rice is tender and the water has been absorbed. Cover to keep warm.

Put the turkey, remaining garlic clove, breadcrumbs, egg and seasoning in a food processor and whizz until thoroughly mixed. Shape the mixture into walnut-sized balls. Heat a tablespoon of oil in a large frying-pan, add the turkey balls and cook them for 13–15 minutes over a moderate heat, turning now and again, until they are cooked through and golden brown.

Heat 2 tablespoons of oil in a pan, add the leeks and cook for 2 minutes. Slice two carrots and add them to the leeks, with the garam masala. Cook for a further 4 minutes, stirring occasionally.

Grate the remaining carrot. Mix 1 tablespoon of oil with plenty of seasoning and pour it over the grated carrot.

Add the cream and tomato purée to the turkey balls and heat through for 1 minute. Pile the rice on a serving plate, top with the turkey balls and cream sauce. Spoon the leeks and carrots around the edge. Serve the grated carrot salad separately.

READY STEADY COOK Tip

• *Minced turkey is economical and delicious and low in saturated fat. Try substituting it for beef mince for a change in a variety of dishes, for example, chilli con carne. You don't have to confine it to dishes with creamy sauces.*

RICHARD CAWLEY

COUSCOUS WITH SPATCHCOCKED QUAIL

The family of Tracey Burgess, from Rushden, Northants, all love food and are happy to try anything new. Tracey brought some quail for Richard to cook, which she thought would be an interesting alternative to chicken, and Richard thought up this way of spatchcocking quail with two skewers and serving it with couscous, as a change from rice, and raw and cooked vegetables.

SERVES 2	4 celery sticks, 2 chopped, 2 sliced thinly
2 quails	600 ml (1 pint) chicken stock
Juice of 1 lime	6 tomatoes, cut into small wedges
1 tablespoon soy sauce	50 g (2 oz) sultanas
1 tablespoon clear honey	25 g (1 oz) butter
1 tablespoon sesame oil	175 g (6 oz) couscous
Tabasco sauce	A small handful of fresh chives, snipped in
2 garlic cloves, crushed	2.5 cm (1 in) lengths
2 tablespoons sunflower oil	Salt and freshly ground black pepper
1 onion, chopped	Fresh chives, to garnish

Using kitchen scissors, cut along both sides of the backbone of each quail and remove the backbone. Open out the quails and flatten them with the heel of your hand. Push two 20 cm (8 in) skewers diagonally through each quail. (If using bamboo skewers, soak them in water for at least 30 minutes, to stop them from burning during cooking.)

Mix the lime juice, soy sauce, honey, sesame oil, a few drops of Tabasco sauce, 1 crushed garlic clove and seasoning. Put the quails on a grill rack and brush over half of the lime-juice mixture. Cook under a moderately hot grill for 12–15 minutes, turning once.

Meanwhile, heat the oil in a pan, add the onion, chopped celery and remaining garlic clove and cook for 3 minutes. Add 150 ml

(5 fl oz) stock, three-quarters of the tomatoes, the sultanas, a few more drops of Tabasco sauce and seasoning. Simmer for 5 minutes.

Melt the butter in a pan, add the couscous, the rest of the stock and seasoning. Bring to the boil and simmer for 3–4 minutes, until the couscous is light and fluffy.

Make a salad with the sliced celery, remaining tomatoes and the snipped chives. Drizzle over the remaining marinade mixture as a dressing and toss everything together. Put the cooked vegetables on a serving plate and add the couscous. Top with the grilled quail and garnish with fresh chives. Serve with the salad.

RICHARD CAWLEY

VIV'S HIGHLAND FLING

Venison steak in a white-wine and mustard sauce, on a bed of potato and marrow

Viv Fetherston's family have been on a low-fat diet since her husband's heart attack. She brought along venison as a real treat for him.

SERVES 2

2 x 225 g (8 oz) venison steaks
3 tablespoons olive oil
1 onion, finely chopped
75 ml (3 fl oz) white wine
1 teaspoon butter
1 teaspoon Dijon mustard
1 teaspoon honey
$\frac{1}{2}$ teaspoon Worcestershire sauce
2 teaspoons Greek yoghurt
1 potato, peeled and diced

$\frac{1}{4}$ marrow, seeded, cut in 5 mm ($\frac{1}{4}$ in) slices and then in fine strips
2 sprigs of fresh rosemary
1 tablespoon chopped fresh parsley

FOR THE SALAD
400g (14 oz) tin of haricot beans, drained
1 garlic clove, finely chopped
1 tablespoon chopped fresh mint
1 tablespoon chopped fresh dill
Juice of $\frac{1}{2}$ orange

Cover the venison steak in cling film and flatten it with a rolling pin; then cut it in 5 mm (¼ in) strips. Heat a tablespoon of the olive oil in a frying-pan, add the venison and sear on both sides over a high heat for about 3–4 minutes for each side. Remove and put in a casserole dish and keep warm.

Using the same pan, add half of the onion and fry in the leftover venison juices, pour in the wine and reduce it. Add the butter, Dijon mustard, honey, Worcestershire sauce and cook for 3–4 minutes. Finally, stir in the Greek yoghurt and a little water and reduce for a further 2–3 minutes.

Meanwhile, heat the remaining oil in a wok, add the potato and marrow, half of the remaining onion, the rosemary and parsley and stir-fry until softened.

For the side salad, mix together the haricot beans, remaining onion, garlic, mint, dill and juice of the orange in a bowl. To serve, lay the venison on a bed of potato and marrow and pour the sauce over. Serve the salad separately.

READY STEADY COOK Tips

• *If you can't get venison steak, this would work just as well using fillet steak.*

• *Try another kind of bean in the salad: there are many kinds available in cans for convenience, such as cannellini beans, kidney beans and chick-peas.*

• *Flattening the meat with a rolling pin helps to tenderise it, which is helpful when you are only going to cook it for a brief time.*

PATRICK ANTHONY

JULIE'S ALPINE JOY

Cheese-topped chicken with salsify sauce

Julie Ritzman now lives in Lufingen, Switzerland, but she enjoys *Ready Steady Cook* via the World Service. Julie brought along some Swiss cheese and salsify, a vegetable that tastes a little like asparagus, in search of new ways to impress her Swiss husband and three children.

SERVES 2	2 boneless, skinless chicken breasts
25 g (1 oz) butter	1 tablespoon sunflower oil
25 g (1 oz) plain flour	100 g (4 oz) Emmenthal cheese, grated
300 ml (10 fl oz) milk	1 onion, sliced in thin rings
400 g (14 oz) tin of salsify, drained, or	225 g (8 oz) broccoli, cut into florets
asparagus or turnips, blanched until tender	1 tablespoon chopped fresh parsley (optional)
crisp and diced	Salt and freshly ground black pepper
1 tablespoon chopped fresh dill	

Pre-heat the oven to gas mark 6, 200°C (400°F). Whisk together the butter, flour and milk in a pan to make a white sauce. Bring to boil and leave to simmer for 6 minutes, stirring occasionally, to let the flour cook out and the sauce thicken. Add the salsify, or asparagus or turnips, and dill and cook until the salsify has warmed through.

Bash the chicken breasts with a rolling pin, to tenderize them. Season the chicken breasts. Heat the oil and fry the chicken for 5 minutes on each side. Transfer the chicken to a shallow casserole dish and bake for 8–10 minutes. Sprinkle the cheese over the chicken and put it under a hot grill, until the cheese has melted and turned golden brown.

Meanwhile, sauté the onion rings in the pan in which the chicken was fried for 6–8 minutes, until they begin to caramelize. Boil or steam the broccoli florets, until just tender.

To serve, garnish a plate with the broccoli. Arrange the chicken breasts in the centre, with the onions on top, and surround with the salsify in white sauce. Garnish with chopped parsley, if you like.

RICHARD CAWLEY

CHICKEN AVE MARIA

Fried chicken with bulghar wheat and tomato and orange salad

Abby Arnold, from Walsall, West Midlands, is a student at Oxford University, a member of a choral group and a keen cook. She brought along chicken, spices and bulghar wheat, in the hope that Richard would create an interesting dish.

SERVES 2	1 onion
2 large chicken thighs	1 green pepper, seeded
2 tablespoons plain flour	1 garlic clove, crushed
1 teaspoon ground cumin	$\frac{1}{2}$ fresh green chilli, seeded and chopped
1 teaspoon ground cinnamon	6 tomatoes, chopped
A pinch of cayenne pepper	3 tablespoons white wine
1 egg, beaten	25 g (1 oz) sultanas
100 g (4 oz) plus 6 tablespoons bulghar wheat	1 orange, peeled and sliced
4 tablespoons olive oil	Salt and freshly ground black pepper
750 ml (1$\frac{1}{4}$ pint) chicken stock	Sprigs of coriander, to garnish

Cut half-way through each chicken thigh and open it out. Mix the flour, $\frac{1}{2}$ teaspoon of cumin, $\frac{1}{2}$ teaspoon of cinnamon, the cayenne pepper and seasoning. Coat the chicken thighs in the seasoned flour and then dip them in the beaten egg. Coat with the 6 tablespoons of bulghar wheat. Heat 2 tablespoons of oil in a frying-pan, add the chicken and cook over a moderate heat for 15 minutes, turning now and again, until cooked through.

Put the stock in a pan and bring it to the boil. Add the 100 g (4 oz) bulghar wheat and simmer for 10 minutes.

Chop half of the onion and three-quarters of the green pepper. Heat a tablespoon of oil in a pan, add the chopped onion and pepper, garlic and chilli and cook for 3 minutes. Stir in the remaining cumin and cinnamon and cook for a minute. Add two-thirds of the chopped tomatoes, the wine, sultanas and seasoning and cook for 5 minutes.

Finely slice the rest of the onion and green pepper. Mix with the remaining chopped tomatoes and put in a salad bowl. Arrange the orange slices around the edge. Season the salad and drizzle over a tablespoon of oil.

Drain the bulghar wheat and pile it in the centre of two serving plates. Put the chicken on top and spoon the vegetable stew around the edge. Garnish with sprigs of coriander. Serve with the salad.

PATRICK ANTHONY

WENDY'S CHICKEN-LIVER DOUBLE DELIGHT

Chicken livers are inexpensive, nutritious and delicious. Supermarket checkout-operator Wendy Hunt, from Swindon, had never tasted or cooked with them, so Patrick showed her not just one but two delicious ideas for using them: in a creamy sauce with pasta and in a warm salad with crisp bacon.

SERVES 2

FOR THE PASTA DISH
6 'nests' or 175 g (6 oz) multicoloured tagliatelle
1 tablespoon olive oil
1 red onion, chopped
1 tablespoon sunflower oil
225 g (8 oz) chicken livers, trimmed, ½ finely chopped, ½ cut in bite-sized pieces
1 garlic clove, finely chopped
2 tablespoons white wine vinegar
120 ml (4 fl oz) double cream

FOR THE WARM SALAD
2 rashers smoked back bacon, chopped
1 tablespoon balsamic vinegar
1 tablespoon olive oil
½ small round lettuce
4 radicchio leaves
½ small ripe avocado, peeled and cubed
5 yellow or red cherry tomatoes, quartered
¼ small cucumber, cut in ribbons
Salt and freshly ground black pepper
Sprigs of flatleaf parsley, to garnish

For the pasta dish, cook the pasta according to the instructions on the packet. Drain, toss in the olive oil and keep warm.

Sauté the onion in the sunflower oil for 2 minutes, until the onions become translucent. Add the chopped chicken livers, garlic and white wine vinegar. Stir-fry briskly for 4 minutes, then season and add the cream to heat through and reduce slightly.

Serve the tagliatelle on a platter, with the creamy chicken-liver sauce.

For the warm salad, fry the chicken-liver pieces, bacon and balsamic vinegar in a tablespoon of olive oil. Season and cook for 4–5 minutes.

To serve, tear up the lettuce leaves and arrange them on a platter, with the radicchio leaves, avocado, tomatoes and cucumber. Spoon the livers and bacon in the centre of the salad and garnish with flatleaf parsley sprigs.

READY STEADY COOK Tips

• *Always trim chicken livers, to remove any tubes and any greenish parts, which may have a bitter taste. Be careful not to overcook chicken livers; they should only just cook through or they will be tough and unpalatable.*

• *Warm salads make excellent light meals when you want something quick but don't feel like a plate of completely cold food. They are also good dinner-party starters, as you can make a small amount of an expensive ingredient, such as scallops or duck livers, go a long way.*

PATRICK ANTHONY

RITA'S REMARKABLE RABBIT

Rabbit with Stilton sauce and fried potatoes

Rita Burton has always wanted to learn how to cook rabbit. She and her husband, Ted, who live in High Wycombe, Bucks, don't like boring food, so Patrick thought up this delicious bacon and Stilton sauce, which will really bring out the delicate flavour of rabbit, served with crisp, deep-fried potatoes.

SERVES 2

350 g (12 oz) skinless, boneless rabbit portions
3 tablespoons sunflower oil
½ teaspoon dried oregano
15 g (½ oz) butter
1 small onion, finely chopped
50 g (2 oz) unsmoked back bacon, cubed
4 tablespoons double cream

50 g (2 oz) Stilton cheese, crumbled
1 tablespoon soy sauce
Oil for deep-frying
350 g (12 oz) potatoes, cut in 2 cm (¾ in) cubes
2 carrots
1 tablespoon chopped fresh coriander
Salt and freshly ground black pepper
Sprigs of flatleaf parsley and chives, to garnish

Put the rabbit portions between two sheets of foil or cling film and beat them with a rolling pin until they are just 5 mm (¼ in) thick. Season with pepper and fry in 2 tablespoons of oil for 8 minutes, until cooked through, turning once half-way. Season with salt and oregano.

Meanwhile, heat the remaining tablespoon of oil and the butter in a frying-pan, add the onion and bacon and cook for 5 minutes. Stir in the cream, Stilton, soy sauce and black pepper and simmer for 2 minutes.

Heat the oil for deep-frying to 190°C (375°F). Deep-fry the potatoes for 3 minutes, until golden and tender. Drain on absorbent kitchen paper. Cut the carrots into ribbons with a vegetable peeler and blanch them in a pan of boiling water for 2 minutes. Drain and season well.

To serve, put the rabbit on a plate and pour over the Stilton sauce. Put the potatoes and carrots around the rabbit, sprinkle coriander over the carrots and garnish with sprigs of parsley and chives.

PATRICK ANTHONY

SANDRA'S CHILLI SENSATION

Turkey chilli with tortillas, re-fried beans and yoghurt-chilli dip

A lover of spicy food, Sandra Wisden brought along kidney beans and soft tortillas in the hope that Patrick would create a chilli recipe with a difference. Patrick obliged with this delicious recipe using turkey as an alternative to minced beef and intriguingly flavoured with cocoa powder.

SERVES 2

FOR THE RE-FRIED BEANS
40 g (1½ oz) butter
400 g (14 oz) tin of red kidney beans, drained
1 teaspoon ground cumin
¼ teaspoon hot chilli powder

FOR THE CHILLI
1 tablespoon sunflower oil
15 g (½ oz) butter
2 spring onions, sliced
½ green pepper, seeded and chopped
200 g (7 oz) tin of chopped tomatoes
1 tablespoon tomato purée
225 g (8 oz) turkey-breast stir-fry strips

1 teaspoon ground cumin
¼ teaspoon hot chilli powder
1 teaspoon dried oregano
½ teaspoon cocoa powder
3 tablespoons double cream
2 teaspoons lemon juice
Salt and freshly ground black pepper

TO SERVE
4 spring onions
150 g (5 oz) Greek yoghurt
1 tablespoon chopped pickled green jalapeño chillies
6 soft flour tortillas
Sprigs of flatleaf parsley, to garnish

Cut 5 cm (2 in) from the base of the four spring onions from the garnish and, leaving the root end intact, thinly slice each one lengthways. Put the pieces in a bowl of iced water and set them aside, to curl.

Melt 40 g (1 ½ oz) of butter in a pan, add the kidney beans and mash them with a potato masher until they are almost smooth. Stir in a teaspoon of cumin, ¼ teaspoon of chilli powder and seasoning and cook gently for 10 minutes, stirring frequently.

Meanwhile, heat the oil and 15 g (½ oz) butter in a frying-pan, add the sliced onions and green pepper and cook for 2 minutes. Stir in the chopped tomatoes and tomato purée and then push to one side of the frying-pan. Add the turkey to the other side of the frying-pan and stir in the remaining cumin and chilli, the oregano, cocoa powder and seasoning. Cook for 3 minutes and then stir the turkey and vegetables together and cook for 8–10 minutes.

Mix the yoghurt and jalapeños together and spoon into a serving bowl. Heat the tortillas, one at a time, in a hot, dry frying-pan for 1–2 minutes, turning once.

Stir the cream and lemon juice into the turkey chilli and cook for 1 minute. To serve, fold two of the tortillas in quarters and put them on the side of a serving plate. Fold under the edges of another tortilla and put it in the centre of the plate. Spoon half of the turkey chilli on top of the middle tortilla and spoon two heaps of the re-fried beans next to the quartered tortillas. Repeat with the second serving plate. Garnish with the spring onion curls and sprigs of flatleaf parsley.

READY STEADY COOK Tips

• *You can use soured cream instead of the double cream and lemon juice, if you like.*

• *Chocolate is a traditional flavouring in South American savoury dishes. It doesn't make the dish sweet but adds a rich depth to the savoury flavours.*

PATRICK ANTHONY

PATRICIA'S SCRUMPY CHRISTMAS

Pasta with chicken and cider sauce, and carrot puffs

On a programme close to Christmas, Patricia Thornborough, from the Isle of Wight, produced some locally made cider, which Patrick used in a delicious sauce for chicken served with pasta. He also made golden, crisp, deep-fried carrot puffs, accompanied by a tangy dip.

SERVES 2

FOR THE CARROT PUFFS
2 carrots, grated
1 leek, halved lengthways and finely sliced, or
4 spring onions, finely chopped
2 tablespoons plain flour
1 teaspoon baking powder
2 eggs, beaten
$\frac{1}{4}$ teaspoon chilli powder

FOR THE DIP
4 tablespoons mayonnaise
2 teaspoons tomato ketchup
$\frac{1}{2}$ teaspoon Worcestershire sauce
A few drops of Tabasco sauce

FOR THE CHICKEN WITH PASTA
Oil for deep-frying
175 g (6 oz) egg and spinach tagliatelle
2 tablespoons sunflower oil
350 g (12 oz) boneless, skinless chicken breasts, cut in 5 cm (2 in) chunks
150 ml (5 fl oz) scrumpy or dry cider
1 tablespoon wholegrain or garlic mustard
15 g ($\frac{1}{2}$ oz) butter
1 leek, halved lengthways and finely sliced
75 g (3 oz) button mushrooms, sliced
75 ml (3 fl oz) double cream
Salt and freshly ground black pepper
Fresh chives, to garnish

Put all the ingredients for the carrot puffs in a bowl and season. Mix well; then set aside. For the dip, mix the mayonnaise, tomato ketchup, Worcestershire sauce, Tabasco sauce and seasoning, to make a dip. Spoon into a serving bowl and set aside.

Heat the oil for deep-frying to 190°C (375°F). Add heaped teaspoonsful of the carrot mixture to the hot oil and deep-fry them for 1–2 minutes, until they are puffed up and golden. Drain on kitchen paper and keep hot while cooking the rest of the carrot puffs.

Cook the tagliatelle in a pan of boiling water for 8–10 minutes. Heat a tablespoon of oil in a frying-pan, add the chicken and cook for 8 minutes, turning occasionally. Add the cider, mustard and seasoning and simmer for 5 minutes.

Melt the butter and remaining tablespoon of oil in a pan, add the rest of the leeks and cook for 3 minutes. Add the mushrooms and cook for 2 minutes. Add the leeks and mushrooms to the chicken, with the cream, and leave to simmer for 2 minutes.

Serve the carrot puffs with the mayonnaise dip, garnished with fresh chives. Serve the scrumpy chicken with the tagliatelle.

READY STEADY COOK Tips

• *Always check that pasta is cooked perfectly by biting a piece: it should be tender but still have a slight bite to it in the centre. The Italians call this 'al dente'.*

• *Cider can be used instead of white wine in a lot of recipes. It goes very well with pork as well as chicken and, of course, with anything with apples.*

MEAT DISHES

RICHARD CAWLEY

STEAK MOTHER ABBESS

Steak with red-wine sauce, mashed potatoes and spinach

Dorothy Bell, from Bradford, is famous locally for her role as Mother Abbess in *The Sound of Music*, so Richard christened this recipe for her favourite food, fillet steak, in her honour.

SERVES 2

350 g (12 oz) potatoes, cut in 1 cm (½ in) cubes	1 teaspoon Worcestershire sauce
40 g (1½ oz) butter	¼ teaspoon English mustard
1 tablespoon sunflower oil	2 x 100 g (4 oz) fillet steaks
1 onion, chopped	225 g (8 oz) spinach, washed and stalks removed
1½ teaspoon cornflour	1 tablespoon olive oil
150 ml (¼ pint) red wine	1 beefsteak tomato, chopped
250 ml (8 fl oz) beef stock	1 tablespoon mayonnaise
	Salt and freshly ground black pepper

Cook the potatoes in boiling, salted water for 10 minutes, until tender.

Heat 15 g (½ oz) of the butter and the sunflower oil in a frying-pan and cook the onion for 5 minutes, until golden. Put half of the fried onion in another pan, stir in the cornflour and cook for 2 minutes, stirring until golden. Gradually add the wine, stirring all the time. Add the stock, Worcestershire sauce, mustard and seasoning. Bring to the boil, stirring, and then leave to simmer for 10 minutes.

Season the steaks and cook them in a hot griddle pan for 6–8 minutes, turning once. Add the spinach to the remaining onion in the frying-pan and cook for 3 minutes, until wilted.

Heat the olive oil in a pan, add the tomato and cook for 2 minutes. Drain the potatoes and mash with the remaining butter, mayonnaise and salt and pepper. Stir in the chopped tomato.

To serve, pile the mashed potatoes on to serving plates, with the steak and spinach. Spoon the sauce around the steak.

R I C H A R D   C A W L E Y

SPOOKY SOUP WITH GORY GARNISH

Pumpkin soup with sandwiches and ketchup

For this programme close to Hallowe'en, Richard made a treat for May Whitehead, from Oldham, who has a passion for ballroom dancing. May had brought a seasonal pumpkin with her, which Richard made into soup, accompanied by cheese and ham 'toasties'.

SERVES 4

FOR THE SOUP
700 g (1½ lb) pumpkin flesh, cut in 2 cm (¾ in) chunks
3 tablespoons soy sauce
2 tablespoons water
1 tablespoon sunflower oil
25 g (1 oz) butter
1 large onion, chopped
600 ml (1 pint) chicken or vegetable stock

FOR THE SANDWICHES
25 g (1 oz) butter
8 slices of bread
225 g (8 oz) Cheddar cheese, grated
100 g (4 oz) sliced ham
Salt and freshly ground black pepper
Sprigs of flatleaf parsley, to garnish
Tomato ketchup, to serve (optional)

Put the pumpkin in a microwave-proof bowl, with the soy sauce and water. Cover with cling film, pierce and cook in the microwave on full power for 5 minutes. Shake the bowl and cook on full power for another 3–5 minutes.

Heat the oil and butter in a large frying-pan, add the onion and cook for 8 minutes, until golden. Put two-thirds of the onion in a food processor with a third of the stock and whizz until finely chopped. Put the rest of the onion in a bowl and set it aside. Add the pumpkin and cooking liquid to the food processor, with the rest of the stock, season and whizz to a chunky soup.

Butter the slices of bread on one side and then, with the buttered side out, make four sandwiches with the grated cheese and ham.

Fry the sandwiches in batches in the frying-pan used to cook the onions, for 4–5 minutes, until golden, turning once. Alternatively, cook in a sandwich toaster. Cut each fried sandwich into quarters, garnish with sprigs of parsley and serve with tomato ketchup, if you like.

Ladle the pumpkin soup into bowls and scatter the rest of the onions over the top before serving.

RICHARD CAWLEY

ALISON'S SAUCY BARBECUE

Drumsticks and sausages with barbecue sauce and corn relish

According to the sons of Alison Sutherland, from Ipswich, Suffolk, her sausages are always a disaster on the barbecue and come out 'like black torpedoes'. Richard showed her how to cook sausages and chicken drumsticks on the barbecue or in the kitchen, with an easy barbecue sauce to accompany them.

SERVES 2
4 chicken drumsticks
6 sausages

FOR THE BARBECUE SAUCE
6 garlic cloves, 2 chopped, 4 sliced
2 tablespoons olive oil
2 tablespoons white wine vinegar
2 tablespoons white wine
2 tablespoons Worcestershire sauce
2 tablespoons tomato ketchup
Tabasco sauce
½ tablespoon water

FOR THE CORN RELISH
1 corn on the cob
½ onion, chopped
1 red pepper, seeded and chopped
2 teaspoons cornflour
2 tablespoons white wine vinegar
½ tablespoon water
2 teaspoons caster sugar
Salt and freshly ground black pepper

Pre-heat the oven to gas mark 6, 200°C (400°F). To make the barbecue sauce, sauté the chopped garlic in the oil for a minute.

Discard the garlic and add the vinegar, wine, Worcestershire sauce, tomato ketchup, a few drops of Tabasco and water to the pan. Bring the mixture to the boil and leave to simmer for 6 minutes, stirring occasionally.

Bake the drumsticks in the oven for 10 minutes. Then baste them with some of the barbecue sauce and return them to the oven. After 2–3 minutes, baste the chicken once again, turn, and cook it for a further 8–10 minutes.

Prick the sausages with a fork. Widen some of the pricks and stuff them with the sliced garlic. Then dry-fry or char-grill the sausages for 10–15 minutes, turning frequently.

To make the corn relish, remove the corn kernels from the cob by slicing down it with a knife. Cook the onion and red pepper in a tablespoon of water for 3 minutes. Add the corn and continue to cook for 2 minutes. In a cup, mix together the cornflour, vinegar and water and then stir into the corn. Add the sugar, season with salt and pepper and bring the mixture to the boil, stirring continuously. Let the sauce simmer until it thickens.

To serve, arrange the chicken and sausages on a plate. Serve the barbecue sauce and corn relish as accompaniments.

READY STEADY COOK Tips

• *This easy barbecue sauce and the corn relish would also be excellent accompaniments to other barbecued food, such as pork chops or burgers.*

• *'Black torpedo' barbecue disasters are mostly caused by having the barbecue too hot, with too much charcoal. This can also lead to flare-ups and the danger that the inside of the food will be undercooked, even when the outside is inedibly charred.*

RICHARD CAWLEY

BARBARA'S BLACK-BEAN BEEF

Barbara May, from Liverpool, said that her rice always ended up a stodgy mess! Richard showed her how to make perfect rice to accompany a delicious beef stir-fry.

SERVES 2

FOR THE FRIED RICE
100 g (4 oz) basmati rice
1 tablespoon sunflower oil
6 spring onions, topped and tailed and sliced on the angle
2–3 tablespoons soy sauce

FOR THE BEEF
2 tablespoons sunflower oil
225 g (8 oz) frying steak, thinly sliced in long strips
1 garlic clove, chopped

1 red pepper, seeded and cut in 1 cm (½ in) squares
2.5 cm (1 in) root ginger, peeled and thinly sliced
½ cucumber, halved lengthways, seeded and cut in half-moons
160 g (5 ½ oz) jar black-bean sauce

FOR THE GARNISH
1 egg
1 tablespoon soy sauce
1 tablespoon sunflower oil
2 tablespoons chopped fresh coriander
Salt and freshly ground black pepper

Cook the rice according to the instructions on the packet. Drain it. Heat the oil in a large frying-pan and stir-fry the rice with 3 spring onions and 2–3 tablespoons of soy sauce for 2–3 minutes. At the end, add the chopped coriander.

For the beef stir-fry, heat the sunflower oil until very hot. Add the beef and cook for 2 minutes. Stir in the red pepper, garlic, ginger, cucumber, the remaining spring onions and black-bean sauce. Cook for 4–5 minutes.

To make the omelette, beat together the egg, a tablespoon of soy sauce and seasoning. Heat a tablespoon of oil in a small frying-pan and cook the omelette. Roll up the cooked omelette and slice it finely.

To serve, spoon the fried rice into the centre of a platter. Arrange half the beef on each side of the rice and sprinkle the omelette strips on top of the rice.

RICHARD CAWLEY

SPICY SAUSAGE AND MASH

Dawn Richardson came all the way from Cumbria to take part in the programme, bringing with her a locally made Cumberland sausage. Richard used it to make a warming winter recipe, combining it with parsnip and apple mash and a mushroom sauce.

SERVES 2

1 large Cumberland sausage, weighing about 500 g (1 lb)
100 g (4 oz) butter
1 potato, peeled and cubed small
1 garlic clove, chopped
1 tablespoon chopped fresh parsley
3 small parsnips, peeled and cut in small chunks
2 Cox's apples, peeled and cubed
Salt and freshly ground black pepper

FOR THE SAUCE

¼ onion, finely chopped
1 tablespoon olive oil
50 g (2 oz) mushrooms, finely chopped
150 ml (5 fl oz) double cream
1 tablespoon Dijon mustard

Grill the Cumberland sausage for 18–20 minutes under a moderate grill, turning once. Clarify the butter by melting it over a gentle heat in a small pan, spooning off any white foam which comes to the surface. Then carefully pour off the clear golden liquid, leaving any sediment at the bottom of the pan.

Fry the potato in 2–3 tablespoons of clarified butter on a medium heat. Stir frequently to ensure even browning. When the potatoes are golden brown, stir in the garlic and parsley and cook for 3–4 minutes.

Meanwhile, boil the parsnips until they are almost cooked. Add the apple and cook until both are soft. Drain the parsnips and apple and then mash them with a little clarified butter and season the mixture.

For the sauce, fry the onion in the oil. When it begins to brown, add the mushrooms and cook for 3 minutes. Stir in the cream and mustard and bring to the boil. Turn down the heat and leave to simmer until the sauce has reduced by half.

To serve, make a bed of the mashed parsnips and apples, place the sausage on top and arrange the potatoes around the edge. Pour the sauce over and around the sausage.

RICHARD CAWLEY

PORKY THE FUNGI

Pork chops with mushroom and mustard sauce and mashed swede

A self-styled 'domestic goddess' to her husband and two children, Soo Sherratt, from Shropshire, brought along some of her family's favourite pork and mushrooms to be turned into something 'divine' by Richard.

SERVES 2	1 onion, chopped
1 medium swede, peeled and cubed	2 teaspoons dried sage
2 tablespoons olive oil	1 tablespoon chopped fresh parsley
2 x 150 g (6 oz) pork chops	2 small Cox's apples, peeled and cubed
50 g (2 oz) mushrooms, sliced	1 tablespoon Greek yoghurt
85 ml (3 fl oz) double cream	1 teaspoon garam masala
1 teaspoon Dijon mustard	Salt and freshly ground black pepper

Bring a pan of water to the boil, add the swede and leave it to cook for 15 minutes, until soft.

Meanwhile, heat a tablespoon of oil in a frying-pan. Season the chops with salt and pepper and fry them for about 6 minutes on each side over a moderate heat. Add the mushrooms half-way through cooking and stir in the cream and mustard for the last 2–3 minutes.

In a separate saucepan, heat a tablespoon of oil and fry the onion until soft. Add the sage, parsley, a spoonful of the cooked swede and the apples and cook for a further 5 minutes.

Drain the swede, return to the pan and mash it over the heat. Stir in the yoghurt and garam masala.

To serve, place a chop in the centre of a plate, pour over some of the mushroom and cream sauce and surround with the mashed swede and apple mixture.

PATRICK ANTHONY

PORK AND CIDER WITH ROS

Pork slices, with cider and mushroom sauce and sweet-and-sour marrow

West Country specialities – pork and cider – were the ingredients chosen by Rosalind Sims from Bristol. Patrick transformed them into a delicious dish of pork and mushrooms in a cream, cider and tarragon sauce, accompanied by spicy marrow.

SERVES 2

FOR THE MARROW
½ small marrow, peeled, seeded and cubed
2 tomatoes
1 tablespoon tomato purée
1 teaspoon sugar
4 drops of Tabasco sauce
2 teaspoons red wine vinegar
A pinch of ground coriander
½ teaspoon Dijon mustard

FOR THE PORK
225 g (8 oz) pork tenderloin, sliced thinly
2 tablespoons plain flour, seasoned
3 tablespoons olive oil
1 onion, chopped
1 apple, cored and chopped
75 ml (3 fl oz) cider
100 g (4 oz) button mushrooms, quartered
2–3 tablespoons double cream
2 teaspoons chopped fresh tarragon
5 drops of Worcestershire sauce
Salt and freshly ground black pepper

Boil the marrow chunks in a shallow pan in a little water for 3–5 minutes. Drain and return to the pan. Add the tomatoes, tomato purée, sugar, Tabasco, vinegar, coriander and mustard. Leave to simmer for 15 minutes, stirring occasionally.

Season the pork slices, coat them with a little flour and fry them in 2 tablespoons of oil for 5–7 minutes, turning half-way. Set aside.

Sauté the onion and apple in the remaining oil for 3 minutes. Add the cider and mushrooms. Season and cook for 5 minutes, stirring occasionally. Add the pork and stir in the cream, tarragon and Worcestershire sauce. Leave to simmer for 10 minutes.

To serve, spoon the pork and mushrooms into the centre of the plates. Surround with the marrow.

PATRICK ANTHONY

BARBARA'S BUMPER BEEF

Steak in a creamy mushroom sauce, with pasta

Barbara Epstein, from the Wirral, Merseyside, is proud of her three children, two grandchildren and a 'bumper' appetite. Some of her favourite foods appear in Patrick's recipe for steak strips in a creamy mushroom sauce, on a bed of pasta.

SERVES 2

150 g (6 oz) pappardelle (broad ribbon pasta) or tagliatelle
225 g (8 oz) rump steak
25 g (1 oz) butter
1 tablespoon oil
½ onion, finely chopped
1 red pepper, seeded and diced
1 green pepper, seeded and diced

1 garlic clove, chopped
1 teaspoon Dijon mustard
Finely chopped fresh parsley
Worcestershire sauce
75 ml (3 fl oz) white wine
100 g (4 oz) mushrooms, sliced
4 tablespoons double cream
½ Savoy cabbage, finely shredded

Cook the pasta, according to the directions on the packet.

Pat the rump steak dry with kitchen paper and cut it in thin strips. Put a knob of butter in a frying-pan, with a dash of oil (this prevents the butter from burning). Add the steak and chopped onion and cook until brown. Remove the steak and place on one side.

In the same pan, add the peppers, garlic, mustard, parsley, a splash of Worcestershire sauce and the wine. Allow to boil furiously, to remove the alcohol. Add the mushrooms and return the cooked steak; then add the double cream and season.

Quickly blanch the cabbage in a little boiling, salted water.

Pour the sauce on to the pasta and serve with the cabbage.

PATRICK ANTHONY

DEBBIE'S DELIGHT

Pasta with beef patties and tomato sauce, and leeks
with gold-medal sauce

Although traditional Welsh recipes such as Welsh broth and Welshcakes were the staples of Deborah Stoddart's Merthyr Tydfil childhood, these days she prefers Mediterranean-style meals. Some of her favourite ingredients, bought for the occasion, go into Patrick's dish; the gold-medal sauce is so named because its versatility and ease of preparation make it a winner.

SERVES 2

FOR THE PATTIES
225 g (8 oz) lean minced beef
1 egg
Worcestershire sauce
1 teaspoon dried oregano
2 tablespoons olive oil

FOR THE PASTA AND TOMATO SAUCE
225 g (8 oz) lasagnette or tagliatelle
1 tablespoon olive oil
¼ onion, finely chopped

300 ml (10 fl oz) passata
A pinch of sugar
1 tablespoon chopped fresh parsley

FOR THE LEEKS IN GOLD-MEDAL SAUCE
1 leek, halved and cut in half again lengthways
2 egg yolks
1 teaspoon French mustard
1 teaspoon white wine vinegar
100 g (4 oz) butter
1 tablespoon fresh herbs (parsley, chives, chervil), freshly chopped (optional)
Salt and freshly ground black pepper

Put the minced beef into a bowl, add an egg, a dash of Worcestershire sauce and oregano and season with salt and pepper. Work the ingredients together with a fork. Form into small patties on a floured board. Heat the oil and fry the patties on both sides, until lightly browned. Remove, drain and keep warm.

Cook the pasta, following the instructions on the packet.

Heat the remaining oil in a frying-pan, add the onion and fry it until softened. Add the passata and a pinch of salt and sugar and cook until reduced to a thick sauce.

Cook the leeks for 3 minutes in boiling salted water, until just soft.

For the gold-medal sauce, put the egg yolks in a bowl, beat in the mustard and vinegar and season with salt and pepper. Melt the butter, but don't let it get too hot as the eggs may scramble, and whisk it into the egg-yolk mixture. Add the herbs, if using. If you wish to thicken the sauce, set the bowl over a pan of simmering water and whisk it. Avoid adding the white residue from the butter if you can.

To serve, drain the pasta, divide it between two serving plates and pile the meat patties on top. Cover with the tomato sauce and sprinkle with parsley. Drain the leeks, place on the plate and cover with the gold-medal sauce.

READY STEADY COOK Tip

• *The method for making the gold-medal sauce is similar to making hollandaise sauce or mayonnaise. The trick is not to add the melted butter too fast and also to make sure that the sauce doesn't get too hot, otherwise the yolks will become grainy.*

MEAT DISHES

CLAIRE'S TURKISH CREATION

Lamb steaks with pilaff and creamy beans

Claire Jones, from Cardiff, loves Turkish food. She brought along some characteristically Turkish ingredients – including lamb and dried apricots – and asked Patrick to turn them into a Turkish-style treat. Patrick obliged with this sophisticated version of a pilaff, seared lamb steaks and creamy beans.

SERVES 2

FOR THE PILAFF
1 tablespoon sunflower oil
15 g (½ oz) butter
1 onion, chopped
100 g (4 oz) long-grain rice
300 ml (10 fl oz) chicken stock
50 g (2 oz) no-soak dried apricots, finely chopped

FOR THE BEANS
150 g (6 oz) runner beans, cut in 2 cm (¾ in) lengths

75 ml (3 fl oz) white wine
150 ml (¼ pint) double cream
2 tablespoons chopped fresh tarragon

FOR THE LAMB
Olive oil
2 x 100 g (4 oz) boneless lamb leg steaks
Tabasco sauce
Salt and freshly ground black pepper
Chopped fresh mint and sprigs of flatleaf parsley, to garnish

Heat a tablespoon of oil and the butter in a pan, add half of the onion and cook for 2 minutes. Stir in the rice, until coated in oil, and then add the stock, apricots and seasoning. Cover and leave to simmer for 10 minutes, or until all the liquid has been absorbed and the rice is tender.

Cook the runner beans in boiling water for 3 minutes. Drain and refresh them under cold running water. Put the wine and the rest of the chopped onion in a pan and simmer for 3 minutes. Add the cream, tarragon and seasoning and simmer for 3 minutes. Stir in the runner beans and cook for 2 minutes.

Rub a little olive oil and seasoning into the lamb steaks and cook them in a pre-heated griddle pan or heavy-based frying-pan over a moderately high heat for 4 minutes, turning once. Sprinkle over a few drops of Tabasco sauce.

Spoon the rice into two ramekin dishes, press down, and then turn out on to two serving plates. Sprinkle the chopped mint on top of the rice. Place the lamb steaks and creamy beans around the rice and garnish with sprigs of flatleaf parsley.

PATRICK ANTHONY

SARAH'S STEAK SENSATION

Coconut beef curry, with rice and courgettes

Currying steak is an unusual and delicious idea. Sarah Witts, from Welwyn Garden City, Hertfordshire, brought rump steak and Eastern spices, in the hope that Patrick could make a curry delicious enough to tempt her husband, Anthony, to be more adventurous in what he eats.

SERVES 2

100 g (4 oz) long-grain rice

FOR THE CURRY

1 tablespoon sunflower oil
1 onion, chopped
1 garlic clove, finely chopped
1 teaspoon ginger purée
2 teaspoons medium-hot curry powder
4 tablespoons water
350 g (12 oz) rump steak, batted with a rolling pin to tenderize, and cut in thin strips

150 ml (5 fl oz) double cream
50 g (2 oz) creamed coconut
Salt and freshly ground black pepper

FOR THE COURGETTES

15 g (½ oz) butter
2 courgettes, grated
1 fresh red chilli, seeded and finely chopped
1 teaspoon soy sauce
Juice of ½ a lime
Finely chopped red pepper and sprigs of coriander, to garnish

Cook the rice in boiling water for 10–12 minutes, until tender.

Heat the oil in a frying-pan, add the onion and cook for 2 minutes. Stir in the garlic, ginger purée and curry powder and cook for a minute. Add 4 tablespoons of water and cook for 2 minutes. Stir in the strips of beef and seasoning and stir-fry for 3 minutes. Add the cream and simmer for 3 minutes.

Melt the butter in a frying-pan, add the courgettes, chilli and seasoning and stir-fry for 3 minutes. Add the soy sauce and lime juice.

Grate the creamed coconut into the beef curry. Cook for 2 minutes, stirring, until the creamed coconut has melted and the sauce has thickened slightly.

Drain the rice well, spoon it into a ramekin dish, press it down and then turn it out on to a serving plate. Spoon the beef curry and courgettes around the rice. Scatter a little red pepper on top of the rice and garnish the curry with sprigs of coriander.

READY STEADY COOK Tips

• *Creamed coconut adds a delicious creamy texture to dishes as well as the delicious coconut flavour. It dissolves very quickly if you grate it and it's a really good way to thicken the sauces of all kinds of curries and casseroles, if you don't want to use cornflour.*

• *Using strips of tender, lean meat like steak is a good way of speeding up the cooking times of curries; combined with stir-frying techniques, you can rustle up an oriental feast in minutes.*

PATRICK ANTHONY

TRACY'S BARBIE BONANZA

Lamb burgers and meatballs

Minced meat is wonderful for creating unusual ideas for barbecues and because it goes a long way, it is very economical. Tracy Wordley, from Sudbury, Suffolk, had brought both minced lamb and minced beef, which Patrick used for two tasty summer barbecue dishes.

SERVES 4

1 red pepper, seeded and cut in 3–4 pieces
2 teaspoons white wine vinegar
2 teaspoons honey
Tabasco sauce
2 onions, chopped
2 tablespoons chopped mixed fresh dill, basil and chervil
2 courgettes, grated
$\frac{1}{2}$ tablespoon sunflower oil
Olive oil
1 garlic clove (optional)
Salt and freshly ground black pepper

FOR THE LAMB BURGERS

1 French stick
450 g (1 lb) minced lamb
1 egg, beaten
1 teaspoon dried oregano
$\frac{1}{2}$ tablespoon sunflower oil

FOR THE MEATBALLS

225 g (8 oz) minced beef
1 egg, beaten
Tabasco sauce
1 teaspoon garam masala
A pinch of hot madras curry powder
$\frac{1}{2}$ teaspoon wholegrain mustard
1–2 tablespoons plain flour

To make the lamb burgers, use enough white crumb from the baguette to give 2 tablespoons of breadcrumbs. Mix together the minced lamb, breadcrumbs and egg and season with salt, pepper and oregano. Then shape the mixture into four burgers and char-grill them, brushed with sunflower oil, for 3–4 minutes on each side, or longer for well-done burgers.

For the meatballs, mix together the minced beef, part of an egg, 4 drops of Tabasco, the garam masala, curry powder, mustard and enough flour to make a fairly stiff mixture. Form the mixture into small balls and char-grill them for 5–7 minutes. Once the meatballs are cooked, thread them on to kebab sticks.

Place the pieces of pepper under a hot grill until the skin blisters and blackens. Put the peppers into a polythene bag and knot the end. Leave until cool enough to handle and then peel off the skin.

Heat the vinegar, honey and 3 drops of Tabasco in a saucepan. Add the onions and cook until they are caramelized. Add the fresh herbs and continue to cook for a few minutes.

Season the grated courgettes and sauté them in the remaining sunflower oil.

Cut two 5 cm (2 in) thick long diagonal slices from the baguette. Drizzle a little olive oil and rub a cut clove of garlic, if liked, over both sides and toast under a grill. The remaining bread can be used to accompany the meal.

To serve, place each lamb burger on top of a piece of toasted bread and arrange them on a platter, with the meatballs and red pepper. Surround with the onion and courgettes.

READY STEADY COOK Tip

• *If you're not barbecuing, serve the lamb burger with burgerbuns and salad for a main course. Try the meatballs with tomato sauce and pasta shapes.*

DESSERTS

PATRICK ANTHONY

CAROL'S CHRISTMAS FANTASY

Sponge casing filled with flambéed dates and banana, with a creamy, lemony yoghurt topping

Containing a medley of Christmas flavours – chestnut, nuts and dried fruit, brandy and orange – this is an exciting, lighter alternative to Christmas Pudding. Carol Markellow, from South London, wanted Patrick to show her a festive but different idea to finish off her family's Christmas dinner and Patrick obliged with this fantastical Christmas creation.

SERVES 4–6	1 banana, sliced
2 tablespoons unsweetened chestnut purée	6 fresh dates, stoned and quartered
250 ml (8 fl oz) double cream	A splash of brandy
6 tablespoons caster sugar	6 slices of marble cake, ½ inch thick
2 tablespoons chopped, mixed nuts	2 satsumas, peeled and segmented
½ lemon, heated in a little hot water	A few sprigs of fresh mint
250 ml (8 fl oz) Greek yoghurt	1 orange, peeled and sliced
15 g (½ oz) butter	1 teaspoon icing sugar

To make the chestnut cream, stir together the purée, 175 ml (6 fl oz) of the cream and a tablespoon of sugar over a low heat for 4–5 minutes until the sugar has dissolved and the mixture is smooth. Sprinkle the nuts into a dry frying-pan and heat until browned, stirring often.

In a bowl, mix together 3 tablespoons of caster sugar, the juice from the half lemon, the yoghurt and the remaining double cream. Melt the butter in a frying-pan, add the remaining caster sugar, the banana and dates. When the pan is very hot, pour in a splash of brandy. Set light to the brandy to flambé the fruit. Line a bowl with slices of the cake. Spoon in the date and banana mixture, add the chestnut cream and then put a layer of satsuma segments on top. Finally, pour over the yoghurt and cream mixture and sprinkle with the nuts. Garnish with the mint and orange slices and sprinkle with icing sugar.

PATRICK ANTHONY

CAROLYN'S FRUIT BASKET CREATION

These brandy-snap baskets with caramelized fruit served with chocolate sauce are an excellent dessert that look beautiful but take only a few minutes to do. That makes it ideal for Carolyn Hall, from Tyne and Wear, a busy young mum who is usually too busy to cook, let alone entertain.

SERVES 2

FOR THE CHOCOLATE SAUCE
75 g (3 oz) plain chocolate
85 ml (3 fl oz) warm water
3 tablespoons double cream
50 g (2 oz) butter

FOR THE FRUIT BASKETS
A little lemon juice
2 small pears, cored and chopped

2 small apples, cored and chopped
4 brandy snaps
15 g ($\frac{1}{2}$ oz) almond flakes
50 g (2 oz) butter
35 g ($1\frac{1}{2}$ oz) caster sugar
1 teaspoon ground cinnamon
A little shredded zest of orange
A little shredded zest of lime
A little shredded zest of lemon
Fresh mint leaves, to garnish

Pre-heat the oven to gas mark 6, 200°C (400°F). Squeeze a little lemon juice over the apple and pear flesh, to prevent it from discolouring. Melt the chocolate with 85 ml (3 fl oz) of water. When the chocolate has melted, stir in the cream and cook for 2–3 minutes. Then add the butter.

Lay a piece of baking parchment or greaseproof paper on a baking tray. Place the brandy snaps and the almond flakes on this and bake in the oven for 1–2 minutes, until the brandy snaps are flat and malleable. Leave the almonds in the oven for 5 minutes longer, until they are toasted golden brown. Place the brandy snaps over upturned cups to form baskets; then leave to harden.

Caramelize the apples and pears in the remaining butter and the caster sugar. After 4 minutes, add the cinnamon and continue to cook until the fruit has turned golden.

To serve, make a lake of chocolate sauce on two plates. Arrange two brandy-snap baskets on top on each plate. Fill each basket with the caramelized fruit and toasted almonds, and garnish with the citrus fruit zest and some fresh mint leaves.

P A T R I C K   A N T H O N Y

JOANNE'S PANCAKE JOY

Fruit-filled pancakes with raspberry-wine sauce

Sweet-toothed Joanne Wall, from Bristol, had brought some of her own home-made wine and favourite fruit and Patrick transformed them into a Shrove Tuesday celebration pudding of pancakes filled with blueberries, strawberries and pecans in an orange liqueur and raspberry-wine sauce.

SERVES 4

FOR THE PANCAKES
50 g (2 oz) plain flour
1 egg
100 ml (3½ fl oz) milk
100 ml (3½ fl oz) water
25 g (1 oz) butter, melted
Sunflower oil, for frying

FOR THE FILLING
25 g (1 oz) butter
25 g (1 oz) caster sugar
Juice of 1–2 oranges
50 ml (2 fl oz) raspberry wine (optional)
50 g (2 oz) dried blueberries or
prunes, or raisins
8 pecan halves, chopped
1 tablespoon orange liqueur
150 g (6 oz) punnet of strawberries, hulled and
halved or quartered if large
150 ml (5 fl oz) double cream, to serve

To make the pancake batter, sieve the flour into a mixing bowl, make a well in it and break 2 eggs into the well. Whisk the eggs and flour together, add the milk and water gradually and continue to whisk until smooth. Slowly add the melted butter.

To make light, thin crêpes, heat a little oil in a pan. When it is very hot add 2 tablespoons of the batter and swirl it to cover the bottom of the pan. Patch up any holes with more batter. Cook until underside is golden. Flip over and brown second side. Repeat to make three more pancakes.

For the pancake filling, melt the butter and mix in the sugar and the orange juice (use half if using raspberry wine). Stir with a wooden spoon and cook for 3 minutes. Add the raspberry wine, if using, the blueberries and pecans and cook for a further 6–8 minutes. Stir in the liqueur and strawberries and continue to cook for 3 minutes.

Put 2 tablespoons of the sauce on each cooked pancake and fold the pancake. To serve, pour the cream on to a plate and put the filled pancakes on top. Pour the rest of the sauce around the pancakes.

PATRICK ANTHONY

VICKY'S PINEAPPLE VICTORY

It's amazing what a variety of delicious ideas can be generated from one fresh pineapple! Looking forward to summer, Vicky Burns, from Macclesfield, had been on a diet and wanted to give herself a tropical treat.

SERVES 2

1 medium pineapple, skin, spikes and core removed, flesh cut in 2.5 cm (1 in) thick rings
65 g (2½ oz) caster sugar
50 ml (2 fl oz) rum
225 g (8 oz) punnet of strawberries
200 g (7 oz) Greek yoghurt
2 tablespoons icing sugar

45 g (1¾ oz) butter
½ teaspoon honey
3 eggs
5 tablespoons double cream
75 g (3 oz) plain chocolate, melted
175 ml (6 fl oz) milk
2–3 fresh mint leaves, to garnish
Ice cubes, to serve

D E S S E R T S

For the pineapple kebabs, cut a pineapple ring into eight pieces and thread them on to three wooden skewers. Coat the fruit in caster sugar and fry in a dry pan for 2 minutes, until caramelized on each side. Flambé the pineapple by adding 3 teaspoons of the rum and setting it alight.

For the yoghurt sauce, mash two strawberries into 2 tablespoons of yoghurt. Mix thoroughly. Hull and cut three strawberries in half lengthways.

To serve, arrange the pineapple kebabs on a plate, placing a strawberry half on the ends of each kebab. Spoon the yoghurt sauce on the side as a dip.

For the caramelized pineapple ring, coat a pineapple ring in icing sugar and fry in 15 g ($\frac{1}{2}$ oz) of butter in a hot pan for 3–4 minutes on each side.

For the rum sauce, mix the remaining rum with the honey and heat gently for 5 minutes.

To make the sweet omelette, whisk together the eggs, 15 g ($\frac{1}{2}$ oz) of caster sugar and 2 tablespoons of the double cream. Fry in 15 g ($\frac{1}{2}$ oz) of butter for 2–3 minutes on one side only, folding it over to make an omelette.

To serve, arrange the fried pineapple ring, pour over the rum sauce and then place the sweet omelette on top and sprinkle it with icing sugar.

For the pineapple with chocolate sauce, chop the remaining fresh pineapple into cubes. Melt the chocolate with the remaining butter, to make a glossy sauce. To serve, arrange the pineapple cubes on a lake of cream, pour over the chocolate sauce.

For the strawberry milkshake, mix together the milk, remaining yoghurt, a tablespoon of icing sugar and 6 strawberries in a liquidizer. To serve, pour into two tall glasses with a few ice cubes and decorate with strawberries and mint leaves.

YUMMY SCRUMMY FLYING SAUCER

Steamed pudding with caramel sauce

Justine Hammond, from Nottingham, had brought the ingredients for a classic old-fashioned steamed pudding. Justine loves to experiment with new dishes but she said she wasn't too confident with traditional English cooking. Richard showed her this classic steamed pudding, served with a caramel cream sauce, which is made in minutes in the microwave.

SERVES 4

100 g (4 oz) self-raising flour
50 g (2 oz) caster sugar
50 g (2 oz) butter, softened
1 egg
4 tablespoons milk
225 g (8 oz) fresh dates, stoned
2 tablespoons flaked coconut

Grated zest of 1 lemon
1 satsuma, peeled and sliced
1 tablespoon clear honey

FOR THE SAUCE

5 tablespoons caster sugar
1 tablespoon water
150 ml (5 fl oz) double cream

Butter a microwave-proof 900 ml (1 ½ pint) pudding basin or bowl. Put the flour, sugar, butter and egg in a food processor and whizz until the mixture looks like fine breadcrumbs. With the motor still running, gradually add the milk and whizz until the mixture is smooth. Chop half of the dates and stir them into the pudding mixture, with the flaked coconut and lemon zest.

Line the sides of the pudding basin with the satsuma slices and spoon the honey into the base. Carefully spoon the pudding mixture into the basin. Cook in the microwave on high power for 4½ minutes. Leave to rest for 5 minutes.

Meanwhile, gently heat the caster sugar in a small pan. Add the water and continue to cook gently until the sugar has dissolved. Simmer for 2–3 minutes, until the syrup turns to a golden caramel.

Push whole dates on to the ends of four wooden skewers and then dip them in the caramel. Put on a sheet of baking parchment or greaseproof paper and leave to set.

Stir the cream into the rest of the caramel and let it simmer for 2 minutes. Turn the pudding out on to a serving plate, pour the cream sauce around the base of the pudding and decorate with the caramel-coated dates.

R I C H A R D   C A W L E Y

KATE AND RICHARD'S SAUCY TARTS

Apricot and plum tartlets, with fruit brûlée

Kate Wilkinson and her husband Richard, from Warwickshire, were looking forward to celebrating their wedding anniversary and Richard's birthday the following day. Richard Cawley made this easy triple dessert of two different kinds of fruit tart and a fruit brûlée to put them in the right mood.

SERVES 2	8–10 plums, stoned and quartered
100 g (4 oz) puff pastry	120 ml (4 fl oz) red wine
1 egg yolk, beaten	50 g (2 oz) brown sugar
8–10 apricots, stoned and quartered	$\frac{1}{4}$ teaspoon ground cinnamon
120 ml (4 fl oz) white wine	$\frac{1}{4}$ teaspoon ground ginger
100 g (4 oz) caster sugar	A few mint leaves, chopped
Seeds from 3 cardamom pods	200 g (7 oz) tub Greek yoghurt

Pre-heat the oven to gas mark 7, 220°C (425°F).

Roll out the pastry until it is 3–5 mm ($\frac{1}{8}$–$\frac{1}{4}$ in) thick. Brush with the egg yolk and then cut out four 4-inch rounds with a pastry cutter. Bake the pastry circles on the middle shelf of an oven for 8–10 minutes. Allow the pastry circles to cool and then slice each one horizontally.

Meanwhile, for the apricot compote, heat half the apricots in a pan with the white wine, 75 g (3 oz) of the caster sugar and the cardamom seeds. Bring to the boil and then let the apricots simmer for 10 minutes, until the mixture is thick and jammy.

To make the plum compote, in a separate pan, heat two or three of the plums with the red wine, brown sugar, cinnamon and ginger. Bring to the boil and simmer for 10 minutes, until the mixture is thick and jammy, like the apricot compote.

Spoon the apricot compote on to two pastry halves and the plum compote on to another two and then cover each with a pastry lid.

For the fruit brûlée, roughly chop the remaining apricot and plum quarters and put them in two ramekins, with the chopped mint. Pour over the yoghurt, and then sprinkle over the remaining sugar. Place under a very hot grill and leave until the sugar has caramelized.

To serve, arrange one of each pastries on a plate with the fruit brûlée.

RICHARD CAWLEY

EASTER STRAWBERRY NESTS

A sweet tooth and a passion for puddings were amongst the ingredients that Jayne Robertson, from Essex, brought along to a programme broadcast near Easter. Richard made her this springtime treat of puff pastry nests filled with strawberries and cherries and served with caramel sauce.

SERVES 2	120 ml (4 fl oz) double cream
1 packet of ready-rolled puff pastry	75 g (3 oz) dried cherries, chopped
1 egg yolk	10 strawberries, halved
1 tablespoon milk	25 g (1 oz) butter
250 g (9 oz) caster sugar	25 g (1 oz) walnuts, chopped
1 tablespoon water	

Pre-heat the oven to gas mark 6, 200°C (400°F).For the pastry nests, cut the thawed pastry into two 20 cm (8 in) squares. Mix the egg yolk and milk to make a glaze and brush the squares with this. Using a sharp knife, make cuts 2.5 cm (1 in) from the edges, stopping 3 cm (1 $^1/_4$ in) short at two opposing corners (see diagam 1 below). Bring one cut edge over and place along the opposite inside corner of the square and then repeat with the other cut edge (see diagrams 2 and 3). Brush the basket again with the egg and milk mixture. Repeat with the other pastry square and bake in the oven for 15 minutes.

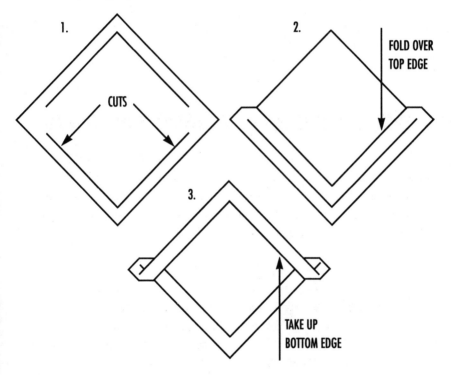

To make sugar shards, place a sheet of foil on a baking sheet. Spread 150 g (5 oz) of caster sugar on the foil and place under a hot grill until the sugar has turned brown, liquid and completely transparent. Check the sugar regularly, as it burns easily. Remove from the grill and allow to cool and harden and then break into jagged pieces of varying sizes.

To make the caramel sauce, dissolve 75 g (3 oz) of sugar in water over a gentle heat. When the sugar begins to caramelize, pour in the double cream, stirring continuously. Any lumps that appear when the cream is added will quickly dissolve. Add half of the chopped cherries.

Sauté the strawberries and the remaining cherries with the butter and the remaining sugar for 2–3 minutes.

To serve, arrange each pastry nest on a plate. Spoon the strawberries into the pastry nest and pour the caramel sauce around the pastry. Garnish with the chopped walnuts and the sugar shards.

RICHARD CAWLEY

DR CLARK'S GINGER PUD

Believing that her dinner-party desserts let her down, Melanie Chown, from West London, hoped *Ready Steady Cook* would provide the answer. Richard saved the day with his simple, frothy syllabub, served with ginger-stuffed lychees, pink grapefruit segments and home-made ginger biscuits. Named after Richard's parents' doctor, who was passionate about these ginger biscuits, this dish will work like a dream.

SERVES 2
400 g (14 oz) tin of lychees
6 whole pieces of stem ginger in syrup, quartered

FOR THE BISCUITS
100 g (4 oz) golden syrup
75 g (3 oz) butter
1 egg
225 g (8 oz) self-raising flour
1 heaped teaspoon ground ginger
A pinch of salt

TO SERVE
150 ml (5 fl oz) double cream
2 teaspoons caster sugar
1 tablespoon grapefruit juice
3 tablespoons Muscat or other sweet wine
1 meringue nest, crumbled
½ pink grapefruit, cut into segments

Pre-heat the oven to gas mark 6, 200°C (400°F). Drain the lychees from their syrup and stuff them with some of the pieces of ginger.

For the biscuits, pour the golden syrup into a food processor, add the butter and egg and blend everything together. Then add the flour, ginger and a pinch of salt and blend again. Put a teaspoonful of mixture for each biscuit on to a greased baking tray (this quantity should make 24 biscuits) and bake in the pre-heated oven for 5–6 minutes, until golden brown.

Whip together the double cream, sugar, grapefruit juice and a tablespoon of wine, until thickened. Fold in the crumbled meringue. Chop a few more pieces of stem ginger and fold them into the cream.

To serve, put four or five stuffed lychees into two tall, stemmed glasses, pour over a tablespoon of wine and spoon half the whipped-cream mixture into each. Decorate two plates with alternate segments of grapefruit, stuffed lychees and ginger biscuits around the edge and put the glasses in the centre of the plates.

READY STEADY COOK Tip

• *With the lychees and ginger, this dessert would be an ideal finale to an oriental-style dinner party, while being creamy and delicious enough to satisfy the greediest dessert-lover.*

INDEX

A

apples,
    sausage and mash 69–70
apricot and plum tartlets, with fruit
    brûlée 87–8
artichoke crisps 19–20
aubergines
    filo pastry boats with two
        vegetable fillings 17–18
    sautéed with stuffed mushrooms
        and cheese sauce 20–1
avocado and chicory salad 22

B

barbecue sauce and corn relish with
    drumsticks and sausages 66–7
beans
    lamb steaks with pilaff and
        creamy beans 75–6
    Thai chicken curry, with lemon rice
        and sesame beans 46–7
    turkey chilli with tortillas, re-fried
        beans and yoghurt-chilli dip
        59–60
beef
    black-bean beef 68–9
    coconut beef curry with rice and
        courgettes 76–7
    meatballs 78–9
    pasta with beef patties and
        tomato sauce and leeks in
        gold-medal sauce 73–4
    steak in a creamy mushroom
        sauce with pasta 72–3

steak with red-wine sauce,
    mashed potatoes and
    spinach 64
beurre blanc sauce with turkey
    escalopes 41
bulghar wheat with fried chicken
    and tomato and orange
    salad 55–6
caramel sauce, steamed pudding
    with 86–7

C

carrots
    carrot and orange salad 36–7
    carrot puffs 61–2
cauliflower and root vegetables in a
    creamy curry sauce 15–16
cheese
    cheese-topped chicken with salsify
        sauce 54
    rabbit with Stilton sauce and fried
        potatoes 58
    soufflés 22
chestnuts
    Christmas fantasy 81
    and cranberry pudding 12–13
chicken
    breadcrumbed with creamy pasta
        sauce 48–9
    cheese-topped with salsify
        sauce 54
    drumsticks with barbecue sauce
        and corn relish 66–7
    fried with bulghar wheat and
        tomato and orange salad 55–6
    in ginger and pineapple sauce
        44–5
    lemon 42–3